# CIRCLES OF FAITH

DAVID G. BRADLEY

# CIRCLES OF FAITH

A Preface to the Study of the World's Religions

78641        BL80.2
          .B81

ABINGDON PRESS     NASHVILLE    NEW YORK

# CIRCLES OF FAITH

Library of Congress Catalog Card Number: 66-15491

Set up, printed, and bound by the
Parthenon Press, at Nashville,
Tennessee, United States of America

TO GAIL

# PREFACE

Although the field of the history of religions is one of keen interest to many persons, it also is a field that, because of its very vastness, presents many difficulties to one seeking to find his way through the maze of information and interpretations. It is perhaps for this reason that the average person is often confused by the claims of various sectarian movements to have the one true answer to the meaning of life, one which transcends the lesser loyalties to any one historical faith, such as Judaism, Christianity, Buddhism, or Islam.

My own interest in writing this introduction to the study of the world's religions stems from my training in biblical theology. The recent emphasis on the peculiar message of the Bible as *Heilsgeschichte*, as the "history of salvation" for all mankind as contained in the story of God's dealings with the Jews and Christians, has led to the desire to relate this biblical claim to uniqueness to the similar claims of other religions. The theme of "circles of faith" is an attempt to examine and clarify this relationship. At the same time each chapter attempts to do several things. Each is concerned with a religious problem or issue which is common to the experience of all men. The problem selected is, however, one which is also important in the field of history of religions. This second criterion has made necessary the inclusion of some material in each chapter which introduces the reader to the religions discussed in relation to the problem under consideration. Although this is often of necessity quite elementary in nature so as to meet the needs of the novice in the field, it is to be hoped that it is never banal. There is a certain amount of information which is assumed to be accumulative as the reader moves from chapter to chapter, but at the same time each chapter stands as a separate unit in so far as it deals with a basic question. Finally, the book is intended to serve only as a preface to help introduce the reader to this important and fascinating field.

I have received much help and encouragement from many friends far beyond that which I can acknowledge here. Professor W. D. White read the first four chapters and offered many helpful suggestions. Mrs. John Blackburn also aided me greatly with a detailed critique of the first half of the book, and I can only hope that I have been able to profit from her suggestions in the second half. Mrs. Jacob Kaplan not only typed an accurate copy of the manuscript but also helped with many suggestions for improvement of style and clarity of meaning.

The book is dedicated with gratitude to my wife, Gail, who has encouraged me continuously and, as always, has been my best critic.

DAVID G. BRADLEY

# CONTENTS

# CHAPTER I

# WE HOLD
# THESE TRUTHS TO
# BE SELF-EVIDENT *

With the entire world going through revolutionary changes
which are without parallel in history it seems doubly tragic
that religion, which should serve and benefit mankind, all too
frequently acts as a divisive factor in our troubled world.
Men of peace and good will who deplore this fact stress the
need for tolerance and harmony. They point out that there
is in our day a special urgency for men of different faiths to
work for greater understanding and cooperation. This is
because all religions are threatened by a common enemy, and
prudence dictates that they combine forces against it. This
common enemy has many names and faces, but usually is
called secularism. In this day of revolutionary change all
traditional ways are under constant attack. This is especially
true in the new nations which have arisen from the shambles
of two world wars and the disintegration of European colonialism. These countries tend to follow the new ways of modern
science and technology in their efforts to break the shackles

* This chapter originally appeared in *The Journal of Bible and Religion*,
Volume XXXIII, under the title, "Religious Differences and the Study of
Religions." It has been revised and enlarged for this book.

of the past and to forge their own destinies. This has accelerated the erosion and undermining of the older ways of the societies of Asia and Africa which usually are intertwined with one or another of the great religious traditions.

Leaders of important nationalist movements in this century —Sun Yat-sen of China, Stalin of Russia, Kemal Atatürk of Turkey, Hitler of Germany, Nehru of India—either have been more or less neutral toward traditional religion or have been violently opposed to it, viewing it as a counterrevolutionary force incompatible with the modern state. Instead, various secular movements, including the state itself, are fulfilling the ancient role of religion. The modern state is essentially a secular phenomenon whether it be fascist, democratic, or communist, and the high priests of religion have been replaced by the politicians and by the men of science, that is, the practitioners of technology and the military tacticians.

### The Problem of Religious Differences

One approach to realizing harmony among religions is to seek a basis for cooperation in the obvious and important similarities to be found in the teachings of the great religious systems of mankind. Some who advocate this approach claim that the founders of the world's religions uniformly have taught brotherly love and cooperation. They decry religious persecutions and wars as monstrous examples of man's selfish actions which are contrary to the true message of all the great religions. Therefore, they say, the present chaos in world affairs would be greatly reduced if men everywhere would recognize the basic similarities of all religions and play down any exclusive claim to final truth. They would have us work in the direction of a world faith which would meet the religious needs of all, and which would serve to bind humanity together into a true brotherhood.[1]

One argument often advanced to support this viewpoint is

[1] Cf. as typical Ruth Cranston, *World Faith: The Story of the Religions of the United Nations* (New York: Harper & Brothers, 1949); David Rhys

based on the recognition that men of different faiths often live their everyday lives in similar fashion. Since this is so, the question is raised as to how important these differences in religious belief really are. By way of example, if one thinks of four men living in the same city block in Honolulu, and working at similar jobs, it would be difficult to tell them apart by outward signs. A Buddhist, Confucianist, Muslim, and Christian living side by side might each eat the same breakfast, ride the same bus, read the same newspaper, and buy the same make of television set with his hard-earned wages. Each pays his taxes and is a decent citizen, even though each professes a different faith. In view of this fact it is asked, why should we not lay aside our beliefs which so often divide us, and stress instead ethical living which is the true heart and goal of all the great religions?

In spite of the appeal of this approach to tolerance and cooperation among men of varied faiths, in fact because of its very simplicity, it is necessary to put up a warning hand. It is worth taking the risk of being misunderstood to insist that we examine carefully, not only the similarities which obviously exist among religions, but the important differences as well. In the area of politics, which has fully as bloody a record as religion, the communist and the fascist each claims to have the only solution for the world's problems, and each is trying to unify the world on the basis of his understanding of the nature of man and of the world's problems. Would one who wants the Christian and the Buddhist to lay aside their differences maintain that it does not matter whether one is fascist or communist? In the United States Republicans and Democrats, advocates of socialized medicine, states rightists, and many other political and economic groups loudly proclaim their positions. Do these positions make any valid difference to their advocates? Birth control, legal control of alcohol, and many issues in the area of morals come to mind

Williams, *World Religions and the Hope for Peace* (Boston: Beacon Press, 1951); Bhagavan Das, *The Essential Unity of All Religions* (2nd ed.; Wheaton, Ill.: Theosophical Press, 1947).

13

as representing positions on which educated, well-informed, and well-intentioned persons have strong, and even violent, disagreements. If it really does matter which position one takes in the areas of politics, economics, and morals, would it not matter all the more in the area of religion which is concerned with ultimate questions about life and death—with the meaning of man's very existence?

Again, when considering the call to worldwide religious unity so as to present a common front to the antireligious forces of rising nationalism, communism, and other secularisms, several further considerations point to the need to include differences as well as similarities in our approach to interreligious cooperation. The problem of religious differences is as old as history itself. Throughout history various prophets and reformers, such as Moses, Zoroaster, Gautama, Confucius, Socrates, Jesus, and Muhammad, led protest movements against the established religion of the day. Yet within a short time these very reform movements usually were broken into sects and divisions. The three missionary religions of our time, Buddhism, Christianity, and Islam, have been spreading their separate messages for a cumulative total of six thousand years, yet today no religion claims the loyalty of even a third of the world's population. And each of these missionary religions is itself broken into many subdivisions and sects.[2]

It is most important to note also that although the leadership of many of the new nations is secular, or even actively opposed to religion, the very development of national pride often leads to a resurgence of traditional faith. In many areas where Christian missions have been strong and active Christianity has been rejected as the white man's religion and as a symbol of colonialism and oppression. In its place has appeared a new emphasis upon the indigenous religion and

[2] For a vivid account of the present conflict among religions, and also of divisions and conflicts within Hinduism, Buddhism, Christianity, and Islam, see Philip Harrison Ashby, The Conflict of Religions (New York: Charles Scribner's Sons, 1955).

traditions of the people, with the result that Asian and African religions are receiving new life and are being followed with pride and vigor. This is an important development and has led to a true rivalry among religions. There is talk of a "post-Christian age," and the missionary activities of Muslims and Buddhists have increased noticeably. In Hinduism the ancient Vedanta is proclaimed across the world as the true religion for all men, Japanese Zen Buddhism is receiving a wide hearing in the West, while Islam is moving forward on several fronts.[3]

One result of this worldwide religious ferment is that even those who advocate the goal of some sort of religious unity must face the crucial question—whose unity? Before a Christian, for instance, can accept the claim of the Hindu Vedantist to possess the knowledge of the true goal toward which all men strive, or take seriously the Buddhist teaching that all sentient beings eventually will attain Buddhahood, he needs to know the grounds of Vedantic or Buddhist faith. At the same time the non-Christian needs to know the grounds for the Christian claim that the gospel is unique. Any approach to an understanding of the world's religions must take seriously the problem of the differences between the faiths by which men live. But this problem does not need to be viewed as a dangerous threat, or as something to avoid, but as a thrilling challenge which we should accept gladly.

### Some Self-Evident Truths Which Distinguish World Religions

Although in their beginnings and primitive forms the phenomena of man's religious experiences follow a common pattern, it long has been noted that the world's religions can be grouped into rough categories according to their different basic world views. Arnold Toynbee, in his volume *An Historian's Approach to Religion*, summarizes the usual point

[3] Cf., e.g., Hendrik Kraemer, *World Cultures and World Religions: The Coming Dialogue* (Philadelphia: The Westminster Press, 1961).

of view by suggesting that there are four possible starting points for a religion.[4] These are first, the straight line view of history found in the Bible and in Islam; second, the cyclical formation and dissolution of the universe to be found in Hinduism and other Indian religions; third, the undulating view of nature and history found in Taoism and Confucianism; and finally, the pessimistic existentialism such as appears in our time in the writings of Jean-Paul Sartre. These four basic standpoints for finding meaning in life practically exhaust the possibilities, and they also restrict the follower of any one perspective or world view to certain limits in his understanding of life.

It is true that the great religious teachers of history asked much the same basic questions about man's life, and sought to furnish fairly simple answers to these questions. In the words of Epictetus, the Stoic philosopher, these may be reduced to the question: Who am I? Why am I here? Where am I going? But the manner in which each religion poses these questions is to a large extent predetermined by the basic assumptions of the world view of that religion. The answers offered by each religion also affect the meaning ascribed to a person's daily experiences. The following illustration of an actual occurrence, and some suggestions as to its possible meaning to persons of various faiths, while not a common experience, may nevertheless serve to illustrate this point.

In the 1930's a story appeared in *The Los Angeles Times* which told of the experience of the driver of a large tractor-trailer on U.S. 99 near Bakersfield, California. The truck was heavily loaded and the driver was making good time. As he droned along in the summer heat he noticed a cardboard box lying in the middle of the road. The driver reported that it was his usual practice to run over such small obstacles with his dual wheels in order to crush them flat and thus remove a road hazard which might prove dangerous for a small car. He stated that he headed his truck for this particular carton in

[4] (London: Oxford University Press, 1956), pp. 20 ff.

order to flatten it when suddenly, for no conscious reason, he swerved to one side, pulled off the highway, went back and turned over the box which he had thus capriciously spared. Inside the box was a two-year-old boy who had crawled out onto the busy highway. He had covered himself with the box and was letting the traffic roar past him. When asked why he had pulled off the highway instead of crushing the box the driver said something like, "I guess God was with me."

When I read this story, what impressed me about the incident and caused me to remember it was the fact that the boy was spared from death. I thought it only natural to read the driver's words that it was God who had been with him and caused things to turn out all right. But the surprising thing is that hundreds of millions of persons in other cultures, with a world view basically different from our biblical tradition, would have entirely different reactions to this event. Although such a person might have the same human reaction that I experienced, that it was good that a child was spared, he would not use the phrase of the truck driver, "God was with me"; or if he did, it might have an entirely different meaning than it would for a Jew or Christian.

Thus a Confucianist (in the classical sense of the term) would have no concept of a creator God who is capable of helping man or even interfering in human affairs. But he would have a strong sense of sympathy with the fact that it was a boy child that was spared. The Confucian system of ancestor worship requires that one have sons to revere parents and ancestors, and a prime cause of the Chinese system of concubinage was the desire to have sons. The loss of a son is a much greater tragedy in this context than is the loss of a girl.

Again, a Hindu might think of the incident in terms of his underlying conviction that all that happens in this present life is due to one's past *karma* (cumulative deeds in previous lives). The sparing of the child, first of all, might be regarded as the fruit of good action in a previous life, on the part either of the boy or the driver. But much more important,

17

the fact that the driver had not been guilty of killing would be considered a tremendous boon. For to take life in any form is bad, and to cause the death of a person is a terrible tragedy since it involves the accumulation of much bad karma which will result in some form of punishment in one's next rebirth.

Many other possible reconstructions of the meaning of this event come to mind, but these must serve to illustrate our main point, that each religion starts with certain axioms or presuppositions, often unconscious, but nevertheless active, which determine how one views the meaning of life. These differing axioms are also to be regarded as crucial, rather than superficial, in that they represent irreconcilable positions. It is not possible to unify the religions of man, nor is it correct to state that all religions are at heart the same. On the contrary it is these very axioms which account for the real differences among religions. At the same time, the apparent similarities are to be ascribed, not to the religions themselves, but instead to the human element common to all men. All men have human sympathies and react in a similar manner to common situations. But the basic questions about the meaning of ultimate issues are viewed from different standpoints which cannot be harmonized. The Fascist, the Communist, and the Democrat may shake hands in the same way and laugh at some of the same jokes, yet they see the issues of politics and economics from radically different points of view. Just as persons of differing political philosophies have differing basic axioms about man and society, so do the adherents of different religions view the world from the standpoint of differing presuppositions.

## Some Basic Axioms of the World's Religions

As was stated above, it is possible to divide the world's religions into three basic groups consisting of the religions stemming from biblical lands, the religions of India, and those which are native to China and Japan. Each group of religions starts with its own self-evident truths, or basic axioms, and within every group each separate religion has its own dogmatic assumptions which set it apart from the others. Let us now take a quick tour of some of the major religions which fall into these broad categories in order to demonstrate this point.

*The world views of Judaism, Christianity, and Islam.* The family of religions which stems from the biblical revelation consists of Judaism, Christianity, and Islam.[5] The sacred writing peculiar to Islam, the Qur'an, is in basic agreement with the major axioms of the Bible, so that it is possible to make a summary statement for all three before each is examined in terms of those individual differences which so far have proved to be irreconcilable. A minimal statement of beliefs common to the three religions might include the following: There exists a God who has created this world.[6] He also has created man and placed him in this world for a purpose. Whatever the vicissitudes of history, God is finally in control of events. This God, who has created the world and guides history for his purpose, will someday redeem or fulfill his purpose for those who trust in him. This he will do by destroying all those in rebellion against his will, and creating a kingdom of God in which all men will serve and please him.

Note that the existence of God is assumed and affirmed, but neither argued nor proven, either in the Bible or in the Qur'an. This world is held to be real, and man's existence in it as divinely ordained. In this basic circle of faith exists a great variety of theologies and interpretations peculiar to each of the three religions, but these always arise from initial common

[5] A fourth monotheistic faith, historically closely linked with three biblical faiths is Zoroastrianism, found today mostly in the Bombay, India, area where it is called the religion of the Parsis (Persians). Although we will include it in a chart of all the world's religions on p. 215 below, we will not discuss the religion as such in this book.

[6] The word "God" presents awkward problems in writing about several religions. It has gained so many emotional connotations in English literature that it has achieved the status of a proper name. In this book when capitalized it refers to the God of biblical religions and no denigration is intended if not capitalized when referring to other gods who usually are mentioned by name anyway.

assumptions whose "truth" is affirmed but never proved and which is usually declared to be self-evident.

The differences which separate Jew, Christian, and Muslim involve certain "truths" which are self-evident to the man of faith within each religion, but which are unacceptable to members of the other religions. These "truths" essentially have to do with a single issue. This is the question of the manner in which God has revealed his will to his faithful followers. For the Jew the New Testament is rejected, and the Christian claim that Jesus was the promised Messiah, or Christ, is denied. Instead Judaism retains the hope for a Messiah who is yet to appear, and seeks to obey the will of God as revealed in the Law, Prophets, and Writings (the Christian Old Testament) and as detailed and expanded in the final depository of divine Law, the Talmud.

The Christian rejects the Jewish claim that the Law is the final revelation of God's will, insisting rather that God's final will and purpose were revealed for man's salvation in the life, death, and resurrection of Jesus, the Messiah and risen Lord. Although the Jewish scriptures are believed to have prepared the way for God's final revelation, salvation is possible only by faith in Jesus as risen Lord.

The Muslim accepts the Law of Moses, the Psalms of David, and the Gospels as revealed scripture, but insists that Muhammad's prophetic utterances preserved in the Qur'an represent God's final revelation to the true believer. Although there was a long line of prophets before Muhammad, and this line includes many biblical figures such as Noah, Abraham, Moses, David, and Jesus, the twenty-eighth and last of the prophets was Muhammad. He is the Seal of the prophets, sent to all mankind. To him was revealed the final message of God, the Qur'an, by means of the angel Gabriel. Although the Jew and the Christian are "people of a book," and therefore to be spared persecution, they do not and cannot have the final truth until they accept Muhammad as the true prophet of Allah, and the Qur'an as containing the final way to salvation.

So far no one has found a way to reconcile these three closely related faiths without starting a new faith, such as the Baha'i movement, a Muslim heresy, which in turn is predicated upon the faith that the message of Baha'u'llah represents the final revelation of the true God for all men, transcending even the revelation through Muhammad.

*The world view of the religions of India.* The view of the meaning of life which is common to the religions of India is in some ways at the other end of the spectrum from the biblical religions. Instead of the belief that each person is a unique creation of God, the assumption is that each of us has been reborn into this world, perhaps many times, before our reincarnation into this present life. Thus one's present existence is but a single link in a series of deaths and rebirths as one passes from life to life. The law that determines one's rebirth is known as the law of karma. This term represents the total and cumulative effect of all one's deeds in all past existences. Whether one is born in high or low estate, or as a man or an animal, is predetermined by his total karma. At the same time it is assumed that this wandering from birth to birth does not fulfill man's true nature; rather, the goal of life is to be found in ending this cycle of rebirths.

It is in the teachings about the nature of the physical world, and of man, his salvation and destiny, that important differences in presuppositions between the Hindu, Jain, and Buddhist views of life are found. For instance, Hinduism, in its main stream of development, is essentially a monism. That is, it is believed that there is only one principle which underlies all that exists. This is the *Paramatman*, or World-soul, which consists of pure spirit or essence and which exists beyond the influence of space and time. Our present world is but an illusory (*maya*) manifestation of this World-soul. The world is bounded by space and time, and these temporary phenomena give the ignorant person the illusion that his soul exists in a meaningful and enduring world. Not only is this maya world transitory; the individual soul also has no permanent individuality but is actually a tiny portion—spark or drop—of the

21

World-soul. Although temporarily trapped in this maya world by ignorance and karma, its true home or proper destiny is to rejoin the World-soul from whence it came. There it will lose its apparent identity as a separate soul and become merged with or absorbed back into the Ocean of Being, the World-soul. Each of the various ways of salvation in Hinduism seeks to aid the religious man in his attempt to yoke (yoga), or link, the individual's soul with the Ultimate.

Another religion whose home is India is Jainism. The founder of this movement, who lived in the sixth century B.C., is known by the title Mahavira, which means "the great man." Mahavira accepted the Hindu presupposition that rebirth is caused by past karma, but he denied that there is a World-soul. Instead his position was that there are two principles, rather than one, which account for this world. This physical world of time and space is real and is formed from one of these principles, ajiva (nonliving), or matter. He taught that there is also an infinite number of separate and eternal souls called jivas (living entities). Although each jiva is, in its natural state, eternally blissful and all-knowing, due to ignorance it can become enmeshed in existence in this world. A person is composed of a soul (jiva) and a physical body (ajiva). Any action one does causes resulting karma to weight the jiva-soul down into existence in this evil world. Salvation and final release are possible only by getting rid of this karmic weight. This is accomplished by strict asceticism and by noninjury (ahimsa, or nonharming). If strictly followed this severe way of life makes possible the freeing of the jiva to its former blissful state far above this world of time and matter.

A third, and very important, religion which arose in India is that of Buddhism, which was inaugurated by Gautama, the Buddha, who also lived in the sixth century B.C. Like Mahavira, Gautama denied that there is a World-soul. Man is not, therefore, an atman or soul whose true home is to return to the Paramatman. Instead (although experts disagree on this) man is simply a "stream of life," or perhaps a purusha (consciousness or person), which endures so long as it is attached to existence by craving or desire. The world in which we live is real, but to exist in this world is to suffer (the first of the Buddha's Four Noble Truths). Life is re-created again and again by past karma, but this rebirth can be stopped if the purusha achieves enlightenment and ceases to think or act as though it were a permanent self. The goal of life is to end rebirth, to cause the false self to wane away (nirvana) so that the fetters which cause the stream of life to continue might be broken, never again to have the power to cause rebirth.

We find, then, that these three religions of India differ from the religions of biblical lands in their presuppositions of rebirth and karma, instead of a creator God with the requirement of obedience to that God. But Hinduism also differs from both Jainism and Buddhism in that in its main stream it is monistic; that is, it thinks of the world as an expression of the Param-atman and of man as having an atman which is a portion of that same Paramatman. On the other hand, both Jainism and Buddhism are dualistic, since they posit a real world inhabited by jivas or purushas. Not only do Jainism and Buddhism differ from Hinduism in their view of man and the world, but they differ from each other in that the first bases its way of salvation upon the teachings of Mahavira, and the second upon the quite different teachings of Gautama, the Buddha.

*The world view of Taoism, Confucianism, and Shinto.* In East Asia we find yet a third basic world view which is held in common by the religions of China and Japan. The "self-evident truths" of Taoism, Confucianism, and Shinto are far more pragmatic and world-affirming than are those of India, and they are far less concerned with an idea of a creator god or revelation than are the religions of the Near East. Instead, these religions usually are characterized as consisting primarily of ancestor and nature worship. Although their world views are far more sophisticated than this simple generalization implies, it still represents a good standpoint from which to survey their common basic axioms.

The beginnings of the religion or philosophy known as Taoism (pronounced *dhowism*) are obscure. The short scripture known as the *Tao Tê Ching* ("way, power, classic," or *The Book of the Way of Power*) is ascribed to the shadowy figure, Lao Tzu, who was reputed to have lived in the sixth century B.C. In this brief book of poems, and also in the essays of Chuang Tzu (fourth century B.C.), we find the expression of classical Taoism which has the following teachings. The natural world, and its inhabitants, all follow a way that is naturally good, and which produces harmony if permitted to follow its own laws. This natural way is called Tao. The entire universe is an expression of Tao, and if it is allowed to function undisturbed Tao will cause heaven, earth, and all creatures to live in harmony. Any attempt on the part of man to impose his own will upon the natural way of the world will lead only to trouble. For instance, to accumulate goods and money for oneself only attracts thieves. To try to govern requires laws, and this leads to wars. The natural way is the good way and is alone to be followed.[7]

This brief statement concerns the world view only of classical Taoism. Although this philosophy was important in early Chinese history, in recent centuries it has subsided into magical practices by means of which the Taoist priest seeks to control the forces of nature for such ends as to yield good crops for the farmer, or to guarantee pregnancy for the securing of sons.

Confucianism is the Western name for the movement begun by Master Kung (551-479 B.C.), whose Chinese name and titles, Kung Fu Tzu, were Latinized as Confucius. Whereas Taoism taught that the troubles of man and society arose when men began to superimpose rules and controls upon the natural way, Confucius began with the assumption that the way of the ancients, the idealized ancestors, was the best way to follow. He and his followers taught that man is essentially good, that the way of *t'ien* (heaven) is to be followed, as it had been by the ancient worthies, and that the prosperity of the nation would be ensured if heaven, the rulers, and the

---

[7] See below, pp. 47-50, for further discussion of Taoism. Cf. Index.

people lived in harmony. Confucius edited the ancient classics and pointed to the ancestral feudal way as one that made for peace, prosperity, and happiness. Man can know what to believe and how to live the best possible life in this world if he but studies the way of the ancient heroes and sage kings of China's mythical golden age as found in the classics. Confucius called himself a transmitter of ancient truths rather than an originator, and his goal was to develop the ideal man in the perfect society by getting men to imitate the past. His concept of the ideal man, the Chün Tzu—literally, "sons of the princes"—is that of the man who knows and does the ways of the ancients.[8]

Thus, even though it is an easy oversimplification, we find that the two terms, "nature worship" and "ancestor worship," do fit these two religions of China, since Taoism teaches that man should follow the natural way as the true way, while Confucius taught that man must follow the way of the ancestors in order to secure peace and prosperity.

When we turn to the islands of Japan we find that the native religion known as Shinto represents a mixture of nature and ancestor worship. The term "Shinto" means "the way of the gods," shin representing the Chinese term (shen) for spirit (god), and to being the Chinese term tao. In its mythology Shinto combines the worship of nature and of ancestors in a manner that parallels Chinese religion but is nevertheless distinctive. In the scripture known as the Ko-ji-ki, "The Record of Ancient Matters," which consists of traditions written down in the eighth century A.D., we read how all that is Japanese is of supernatural origin. The Ko-ji-ki tells how the first gods (or kami beings) later created the gods of nature, such as the sun goddess, Amaterasu, and the storm god, Susano-wo, and also how the two divine beings, Izanagi and Izanami (male-who-invites and female-who-invites), created the islands of Japan. The ancestry of the Japanese emperor is traced di-

[8] See below, pp. 51-52, for further discussion of Confucianism. Cf. Index.

rectly to the gods, as is also that of the Japanese people themselves. Since the Japanese Islands and the whole world of nature, as well as the Japanese people, are of divine origin, the ancient Japanese way is the good and true way; in other words, it is *Shinto*, or *kami no michi*, the way of the gods.

For these three religions of East Asia there is agreement in viewing this present world as both real and good. At the same time each also has its own peculiar presuppositions. Taoism assumes a way of nature which one must learn and follow if one is to find meaning in life. The Confucian idealizes the ancient feudal way, and the goal of individual and social life is to recover the golden age of the ancients. In Japan Shinto ascribes divinity to all that is Japanese, so that true religion requires that one honor as holy both the Japanese Islands and the way of the ancestors.

Here then are three important world views—those of biblical lands, those arising in India, and those of East Asia. It is true that these important positions have been stated somewhat crassly and in such a manner that an expert, or an adherent of any one of the faiths described, would complain that his position was unfairly presented, simply because "there is a lot more to it than you are saying." Apart from the limitations of such a brief presentation, however, it is here maintained that the initial assumptions, the basic axioms of each of these world views are irreconcilable with those of the others. Either there is a God who makes a difference in the history of man, or there is not. Either man is reborn into this world in a series of lives, as is assumed in the religions of India; or he is created as a unique individual, as in biblical religions; or he is descended from ancestors who lived perfectly, as in the religions of China and Japan. Either life has meaning in terms of the purpose of the God of the Bible, or in escape from the cycle of rebirth, or in the following of the ancient ways of China or Japan—or, rather, one cannot combine these different axioms without mental gymnastics that would turn one into a spiritual tumbleweed.

*Circles of Faith*

Contemporary theologians and historians agree upon the subjective dimension of man's attempts to discover meanings in the area of human relationships. Not only one's self, but other persons, cultures, religions, and even the movements of history, are all shown to be understood subjectively as one seeks to select and interpret data in these areas. Thus one might ask who could write an unbiased biography of Adolf Hitler, granting that his autobiography, *Mein Kampf,* involves obvious subjective judgment. Could a contemporary German do so without interjecting his own feeling, pro or con, into his interpretation? Could a Jew who had suffered in a concentration camp, or any of the millions of soldiers whose lives were disrupted by World War II, view dispassionately and with complete objectivity the career of Der Führer? It would not be possible to gather, select, and interpret the facts of Hitler's life so that every reader would be pleased and satisfied with the results.

In the field of religious thought the goal of objectivity is not even remotely to be achieved, at least in terms of finding a starting point for interpretation upon which members of all religions could agree. Can the Christian really understand the world view of the Hindu which is the basis of the Hindu closed system of thought, and in whose framework the caste system, and all the other aspects of Hindu life are lived and experienced? For centuries Christian missionaries have pointed out to Hindus what they thought, from the Christian point of view, to be the shortcomings and weaknesses of Hindu pessimism, only to achieve relatively meager results in terms of converts. Even Hindu women, who should "have nothing to lose but their chains," appeared to be little concerned about their unfortunate plight as seen through the eyes of a Christian. Again, the Shinto concept of the divinity of the emperor is unacceptable to the West. But should not these and many other similar facts help us see that the basic religious systems make mutually exclusive claims and offer divergent solutions to the problem of the meaning of life? No one has been able to explain adequately why these divergent views, based on such radically different assertions, came into existence. Yet this lack of agreement between systems of thought has plagued man throughout his entire history. Men have never been particularly successful in their attempts to get others to agree with them upon the dogmas of religious faith. The Christian cannot, as such, prove the existence of God to the nonbeliever. The Hindu's belief in preexistence in a former earthly life and his doctrine of the transmigration of souls leave the Westerner unconvinced. The Confucian idealization of the Chinese "golden age" would not arouse the enthusiasm of the average American.

Some years ago the editors of *The New Yorker* magazine reported an interview with Dr. Kurt Gödel, of the Institute for Advanced Study at Princeton. This interview concerned Harvard's awarding Dr. Gödel an honorary Doctor of Science degree. The citation read, "Discoverer of the most significant mathematical truth of this century, incomprehensible to laymen, revolutionary for philosophers and logicians." In reporting the interview *The New Yorker* stated:

Dr. Gödel explained that what Harvard had been referring to was his work in proving that mathematics is inexhaustible. "Which means," he said, pronouncing the words slowly, "that for any well-defined system of mathematical axioms there exist mathematical questions that cannot be settled on the basis of these axioms. Clear?" We said we thought we had it, and he continued. "The significance of the findings lies in the philosophical questions they imply. Now, look: Since mathematics is inexhaustible, two alternatives are possible. Either the human mind itself is inexhaustible or the human mind falls short of mathematics—that is, there exist clear-cut mathematical 'yes or no' questions which will be forever undecidable for human beings." [9]

[9] August 23, 1952, p. 14. Reprinted by permission; copyright © 1952, The New Yorker Magazine, Inc.

28

Although there has been no great crisis in philosophy over the findings of Professor Gödel, the above statement appears to strengthen the logic of the position here advocated. Laying aside for the moment the claims to revealed truth professed by many religions and following the approach of human reason and logic which is used by the proponents of a world faith, it is maintained that different religions are based upon different sets of axioms which are used to explain the meaning of life in each of these religious systems.

When Thomas Jefferson composed the Declaration of Independence, the arguments which he included seemed to presuppose that the self-evident truths to which he referred might not have been self-evident to King George III. So too, axioms such as a creator God or the rebirth of the individual soul, although self-evident to the member of a religion, might not be self-evident to those of another persuasion. It also is to be noted that each religion has certain embarrassing problems in connection with its own world view, and, although answers proposed for such problems may satisfy the adherent to the religion, these same answers usually fail to convince the skeptic and outsider. In Christianity, for instance, one begins with the affirmation that there is one true God who has created the world. Our best theologians tell us that it is fruitless to attempt to prove the existence of God even though we need to make consistent sense in demonstrating, from the Christian point of view, that belief in God is true. But belief in a creator God also carries with it the problem of evil, of why a good God can permit evil to exist in his creation. The only sound Christian answer to this problem is one of faith, that one is to trust God in the face of the fact of evil. In other words, we cannot resolve certain questions in Christianity logically, but rather we affirm our faith on the basis of our axioms concerning God and his creation. So too, the Hindu is involved with certain unanswerable questions concerning such things as the apparent reality of what is to the Westerner this world of material things but which the Hindu calls maya, illusory, or his axiom of the fact of preexistence and rebirth which, like the Christian view of the creator God, is unprovable.

If this be so, how are we to study other religions so that we can understand the meaning of others' faiths, thereby also helping further peace and brotherhood in our time? First of all, the usual notion of comparative religions has to be discarded—the notion that one can line up the ten or twelve living religions on a chart, examine each in turn, and arrive at some kind of inductive truth which will satisfy one concerning this problem. The Christian asks questions of Hinduism which are based on *Christian* assumptions; the Hindu asks his own kind of questions about the biblical view of life; and so on. We must remind ourselves continually of the subjective and limited nature of our ability to understand the religious position of a member of another faith.

Immediately the question may arise, "Then, can truth be found?" The answer is that truth can be found only in the context of one's faith, for truth in religion is conviction first of all, and not the result of a process of inductive logic. We are often reminded, by proponents of the scientific search for truth, of Jesus' words in John 8:32, "You will know the truth, and the truth will make you free." If this entire statement is quoted, however, we receive a far different meaning than the implication that the Christian is to seek truth as an abstract good wherever it may lead. What the Gospel here says is, "If you remain in my *logos*—my word—then you shall know the truth and the truth shall make you free." And what is the *logos* in John except the basic axiom of his whole interpretation of the Incarnation, that the *logos* had become flesh and dwelt among us in the person of Jesus, the Christ?

The Hebrew word for "faith" is very instructive in this connection. It is related to the word "amen," which means let it be firm or established. Faith can in this sense be interpreted as meaning one's standpoint, the firm place from which he views the world. If one stands within the circle of Christian faith, he understands, from that standpoint, something of the meaning of the Christian axioms concerning God and his purpose for the world. The Buddhist, on the other hand, has his own circle of faith from within which he views and understands the meaning of his existence. Each can know something of the other's circle of understanding because of common human sympathies, but it would be necessary to step outside one's own circle to be able fully to understand the faith of one who holds a different world view, and this cannot be done since one would then be standing within another circle of faith with the same human limitations unchanged.

Let us then learn to stress in this connection not the obvious similarities, but the profound differences between religions. This could make a very positive contribution to world understanding because it would first of all help us understand better the true nature of our own faith. If it also were to help us take more seriously the bedrock beliefs of those of other religions, then our sincere concern could but lead to better intercommunication and understanding.

This thesis that each religion stands within its own circle of faith and is governed by certain self-evident presuppositions will be applied in subsequent chapters to six areas of thought and action common to the various religions. In each case the basic problem of the chapter will be illustrated by a representative selection of materials from pertinent religions, although it is hoped that this will not lead to suppressing evidence which might run counter to the basic thesis.

# CHAPTER 2

# GOD MUST
# HAVE A NAME

One of the most intriguing and difficult questions in the study of world religions is whether the god in whom one believes is the same god that is worshiped by the followers of other religions. The affirmation of the poet mystic, William Blake, that "All religions are one," is often quoted and is the working hypothesis of many interpreters of religion. The proposition presented by such persons usually has a double aspect. The first part states that there actually is only one true God for all men. To this statement is added the claim that all mankind, whether consciously or unknowingly, is seeking this one true God, though in many different ways. These various ways to the one God comprise the various religions of man.

A corollary to this twofold proposition is that although there are many ways to this God, since each road shares this common goal—all roads lead to the same God—there is no final difference between the religions of men. Each religion advocates a different way to reach the common goal of union or peace with God. God is called by many names and is known in many ways because of his infinite nature. But, say the advocates of this position, only the religious bigot would claim either to have the only true God or to possess the only way to his God.

An excellent exposition of this position is to be found in a book by the late English author Aldous Huxley, entitled *The Perennial Philosophy*. Huxley's view was that the perennial philosophy represents the religious quest common to all mankind and is predicated upon the existence of an ultimate reality, or Ground of Being. In Huxley's words:

Philosophia Perennis—the phrase was coined by Leibniz; but the thing—the metaphysic that recognizes a divine Reality substantial to the world of things and lives and minds; the psychology that finds in the soul something similar to, or even identical with, divine Reality; the ethic that places man's final end in the knowledge of the immanent and transcendent Ground of all being—the thing is immemorial and universal.[1]

This volume is essentially an anthology of religious texts which represents two basic sources. Most of the material consists either of quotations from the mystics of various religions, or else from the scriptures of those religions which subscribe to a monistic or pantheistic position, such as is found in vedantic Hinduism, or classical Taoism. It is interesting that Huxley quoted almost nothing from the Bible (except from the Gospel of John), explaining that this material is familiar and accessible to most of his readers.[2] In actual fact there is not much in the Bible which would support his position. He also sought to prove, or at least to demonstrate, the existence of a Ground of Being, even though many Christian theologians aver that one cannot prove the existence of the biblical God.

Another important representation of this position is the fascinating book by Joseph Campbell, *The Hero with a Thousand Faces*.[3] Starting with the problem of man's existence and

[1] (New York: Harper & Row, 1945), p. vii.
[2] *Ibid.*, p. x.
[3] (New York: Pantheon Books, 1949). Actually Campbell has since modified his position in the direction of the greater distinctiveness of each religion, but this book is an important illustration of results gained by the application of Jungian principles to the study of religions.

assuming a psychology close to that of C. G. Jung, Campbell claims to find a basic myth which is common to all religions. This monomyth is about the Hero, the man who faces the fact of death and overcomes it in heroic fashion. There are no gods except as man has fashioned them, but this archetypal myth of the Hero, to be found in all religious tradition, presents a way for man to find meaning in an alien universe.

Campbell's position, in spite of its ruthless rationalism and hard-headed honesty, is predicated upon presuppositions which basically are monistic. Thus he asserts that just "as the individual is an organ of society, so is the tribe or city—so is humanity entire—only a phase of the mighty organism of the cosmos." [4] And again:

The essence of oneself and the essence of the world; these two are one. Hence separateness, withdrawal, is no longer necessary. Wherever the hero may wander, whatever he may do, he is ever in the presence of his own essence—for he has the perfected eye to see. There is no separateness. Thus, just as the way of social participation may lead in the end to a realization of the All in the individual, so that of exile brings the hero to the Self in all.[5]

This quick look at two excellent expositions of the position that all religions are one, both of which affirm a Ground of Being as the common basis for man's existence, serves to emphasize the gravity of the problem of religious understanding in this crucial area. This chapter builds upon the thesis of chapter one, that differing religious presuppositions lead to the formation of separate circles of faith. This is done by examining the question of "who god is" for some of the important religions of the world, with the intent of considering afresh the basic question of whether all religions have the same god.

### God in the Bible and in Islam

*The God of the Bible.* The position of the Bible on the question of who God is appears to run counter to the point of

[4] *Ibid.*, p. 384.
[5] *Ibid.*, p. 386.

view represented by Huxley and Campbell—that a common "Ground of Being" underlies all religious activity. This is made clear in the story of the real beginning of Hebrew faith in the third chapter of the book of Exodus. Here we read the story of how the God of the Bible first appeared to Moses in the burning bush. As the chapter opens we find Moses keeping sheep in the desert of Midian.

God called to him out of the bush . . . and he said, "I am the God of your father, the God of Abraham, the God of Isaac, and the God of Jacob." And Moses hid his face, for he was afraid to look at God.

Then the Lord said, "I have seen the affliction of my people who are in Egypt, and have heard their cry because of their task-masters; I know their sufferings, and I have come down to deliver them out of the hands of the Egyptians, and to bring them up out of that land to a good and broad land, a land flowing with milk and honey, to the place of the Canaanites. . . . Come, I will send you to Pharaoh that you may bring forth my people, the sons of Israel, out of Egypt." But Moses said to God, "Who am I that I should go to Pharaoh, and bring the sons of Israel out of Egypt?" He said, "But I will be with you; and this shall be the sign for you, that I have sent you: when you have brought forth the people out of Egypt, you shall serve God upon this mountain."

Then Moses said to God, "If I come to the people of Israel and say to them, 'The God of your fathers has sent me to you,' and they ask me, 'What is his name?' what shall I say to them?" God said to Moses, "I am who I am." And he said, "Say this to the people of Israel, 'I am has sent me to you.'" God also said to Moses, "Say this to the people of Israel, 'The Lord, the God of your fathers, the God of Abraham, the God of Isaac, and the God of Jacob, has sent me to you': this is my name for ever, and thus I am to be remembered throughout all generations." [6]

If one takes the position that all men worship the same God, though perhaps by different names, it should be startling to be reminded that in this story Moses wants to know which god it is that has spoken to him. At this point, however, the

[6] Vss. 4b, 6-8b, 10-15.

god of the Bible identifies himself in two ways; he gives his name as the LORD—in Hebrew this is the divine name represented by the four consonants YHWH, probably pronounced Yahweh. He also states that he is the same god who was known to Abraham, Isaac, and Jacob, three ancestors of the Israelite tribes. This revelation to Moses, in other words, is not remembered as merely one more religious experience of the sons of men, but instead is presented as a significant revelation by a specific God who so identifies himself that he cannot be mistaken for any other god.

This insistence upon identifying who God is, and also of warning against confusing Yahweh with other gods, is found throughout the Bible. Thus in the story of Joshua, in the generation following Moses, we have a repetition of this theme in the famous assembly at Shechem. Joshua had called the leaders of the twelve tribes together for a renewal of the covenant which Yahweh had made with Israel at Mt. Sinai. After a rehearsal of Hebrew history from the call of Abraham to his day, in which stress is placed upon Yahweh's continual help and saving power, Joshua concludes:

Now therefore fear the LORD, and serve him in sincerity and in faithfulness; put away the gods which your fathers served beyond the River, and in Egypt, and serve the LORD. And if you be unwilling to serve the LORD, choose this day whom you will serve, whether the gods your fathers served in the region beyond the River, or the gods of the Amorites [Canaanites] in whose land you dwell; but as for me and my house, we will serve the LORD.[7]

Here we note both the possibility of serving other gods than Yahweh, and also the insistence that to serve Yahweh requires the renunciation of all other gods. In this sense the Bible is not monotheistic but rather teaches that other gods are real and can be served. It also insists that a true believer can serve only Yahweh. This necessity of serving only the God of the

[7] Josh. 24:14-15.

Bible is found in both Testaments and runs with undiminished vigor throughout the Bible.

Thus, for instance, the prophetic movement in Israel is founded upon this double principle, and the story of Elijah, the ninth-century B.C. popular hero of the movement, is essentially the story of how he championed the cause of Yahweh against the followers of the Canaanite fertility god, Baal.[8] Amos, writing about 750 B.C., condemned the Israelites for apostasy from Yahweh to other gods, as did his contemporaries, Hosea, Micah, and Isaiah. Even the theology of Isaiah of Babylon, the sixth-century B.C. prophet of the Exile, whose message is found in Isaiah 40–55, and who is sometimes called the father of biblical monotheism, is in harmony with this theology. He labeled other gods as false gods and said that Yahweh is the only true God, but he still admitted the fact that men serve other, false gods though they should instead serve Yahweh alone.[9]

In the New Testament this double theme is continued with unabated force. When Jesus was asked, "Which commandment is first of all?" he replied with a quotation from the Old Testament which is a portion of the *Shema*, or Jewish statement of faith. "Hear, O Israel: The Lord our God, the Lord is one; and you shall love the Lord your God with all your heart, and with all your soul, and with all your mind, and with all your strength." [10] It is not just the philosophical notion of deity that is referred to here; the stress instead is upon the identity of the God of Jesus as being the same as the God of Abraham, Isaac, and Jacob, of Moses and the other prophets, the god whose name is Yahweh, or the LORD. Jesus also seemed to think that it was possible to serve other gods than the Lord, because, like Joshua of old, he called upon his hearers to serve only the one true God.

"No one can serve two masters; for either he will hate the

[8] I Kings 17–18.
[9] Isa. 42–45, especially. See also chap. 4 below.
[10] Mark 12:29-30. This parallels Deut. 6:4 but adds the phrase "with all your mind."

one and love the other, or he will be devoted to the one and despise the other. You cannot serve God and mammon." [11]

The apostle Paul, who gives us our earliest interpretation of the meaning of Jesus as the Jewish Messiah, or the Christ, also admits the existence of other gods besides the God of Moses. He insists, however, that Christians must worship the God of the Jews only, the God who had again revealed his saving power by raising Jesus from the dead. Thus in I Corinthians 8:5-6, in warning the Corinthians against becoming polluted by eating food which had been offered to idols he says: "For although there may be so-called gods in heaven or on earth— as indeed there are many 'gods' and many 'lords'—yet for us there is one God, the Father, from whom are all things and for whom we exist, and one Lord, Jesus Christ, through whom are all things and through whom we exist."

In the same letter Paul takes the position that a religious experience, not unlike the enthusiastic sort associated with the gift of the Holy Spirit, is found among those who do not believe in the biblical God.

Now concerning spiritual gifts, brethren, I do not want you to be uninformed. You know that when you were heathen, you were led astray to dumb idols, however you may have been moved. Therefore I want you to understand that no one speaking by the Spirit of God ever says "Jesus be cursed!" and no one can say "Jesus is Lord" except by the Holy Spirit.[12]

Is not Paul here insisting that one who owns Jesus as Lord is serving another, a radically different, God than one who follows a heathen god, however positive may have been the spiritual manifestations of that false service?

While the Jew and the Christian serve the same God, there is, of course, a basic difference between the Jew and the Christian in terms of how each feels the will of God is re-

[11] Matt. 6:24. To those who would argue that "mammon" represents riches and not a god it must be answered that if one serves riches he is serving a false god.

[12] I Cor. 12:1-3.

vealed. For the Jew God's will was made known through his call of the children of Israel, and his revelation through the law of Moses and the teachings of the prophets. The Christian, although accepting this revelation, believes that God has spoken his final will to man through the life, death, and resurrection of Jesus, who is hailed as the true Jewish Messiah, or Christ.

*The God of Islam.* The religion known as Islam, which was begun by the prophet Muhammad (A.D. 570-632), continues the stream of biblical thought, for this religion accepts both the Old and New Testaments as divinely revealed. But just as Christianity accepts a later revelation than that of the Hebrew scriptures—that is, the revelation contained in the Christian New Testament—so Islam accepts God's revelation through Muhammad contained in the Holy Qur'an as the culmination and seal of God's revelation to man. The name by which Muhammad's God revealed himself is *Allah.* Some scholars hold this name to be an abbreviated form of the term "The God" (*al illah*), while others say that it is the name of a deity known before Muhammad, and thus a term whose origin is obscure. In any case, the God of the Muslim is named Allah and is identified as the God who revealed his will for all men through his prophet Muhammad. Those prophecies and teachings of Muhammad which were uttered in a state of trance and were claimed as divinely inspired were written down in the Qur'an. Shortly after the death of the Prophet a corrected and authoritative edition of the Qur'an was prepared. This book contains all the revelations given to Muhammad; all former revelations are superseded by the Qur'an, and no teaching that disagrees with this Holy Book is true.

The term "Islam" means "submission," and a Muslim is "one who submits," that is, to the will of Allah. The Qur'an stresses the majesty and sovereignty of Allah and proclaims submission to him as the sole way to find peace and salvation. Since Allah alone can save or punish, the true believer must turn to him in complete submission, while the fate awaiting the unbeliever after death is terrible to hear. "Say to the

39

infidels: ye shall be worsted, and to Hell shall ye be gathered together; and wretched the couch!" [13] But more to the point, Allah is not to be equated with any other deity, and "the greatest of all sins is *shirk* or 'association,' i.e., giving to anyone or anything even the smallest share in Allah's unique sovereignty." [14]

Allah, there is no deity save Him, the Living, the Self-subsistent. Slumber takes Him not, nor sleep. His is whatever is in the heavens and whatever is on earth. Who is it will intercede with Him save by His leave? He knows what is before them and what is behind them, whereas they comprehend naught of His knowledge save what He wills. Wide stretches His Throne over the heavens and the earth, yet to guard them both wearies Him not, for He is the High, the Mighty.[15]

Note that the Qur'an does not say, "He is whatever is," but rather, "*His* is whatever is." Allah is not essence but creator, and man is not part of God but is God's creation.

It would appear, then, that the basic teaching about deity in Judaism, Christianity, and Islam runs counter to the monistic position that the same god underlies all religions. Instead, God is identified by name, either as Yahweh or Allah, and is declared to be distinctly separate from other gods of mankind, whether they be the Canaanite Baal, or the Greek Zeus, or any of the other gods of the unfaithful. The God of these religions is creator of the world, not an essence from which the world emanates; he is judge, holding his creatures responsible to his will; he is the redeemer who guides history for his purpose, and who comes to the saving help of his people by such acts as the exodus out of Egypt, the return of Jews from exile, the raising of Jesus from the dead, and the revelation of the Qur'an through Muhammad.

[13] Qur'an, Sura III:10, J. M. Rodwell, tr.
[14] Arthur Jeffery, *Islam: Muhammad and His Religion* (Indianapolis: The Bobbs-Merrill Company, 1958), p. 85.
[15] *Ibid.*, Sura II:256, p. 86.

## The Nature of God in Hinduism, Jainism, and Buddhism

God in Hinduism. The relationship assumed to exist between the god of a religion and this present world of space and time can be conceived in only a limited number of ways. One approach is to affirm a creator God who has made the world and its inhabitants, either out of nothing or out of some coeternal principle. That is, their relationship is conceived in terms of a dualism, in that the deity and the world represent two separate principles or entities. Biblical religion fits this category. Another approach is to think in terms of a single principle which accounts for everything, both temporal and spatial. Since a single principle underlies all that is, this position is usually called monistic. The most profound expression of monism—of affirming a single principle which accounts for all that is—is found in Hinduism.

The religion of the Hindus covers so many ways of salvation, and so many varied philosophical systems, that any summary statement about Hindu metaphysics is less than completely adequate. In America many Hindu apologists are able to make capital of this situation by pointing to errors of fact and misconceptions in interpretation of Hinduism by a Westerner —according to the particular point of view of Hinduism which is held by the apologist. Yet there is a classical expression of Hinduism upon which all later systems build. This is found in the philosophical writings known as the *Upanishads*. As early as the sixth century B.C., when Jainism and Buddhism arose, the monistic philosophy of the Upanishads had taken its basic form. All that has followed in later Indian thought either gives further expression to this world view or else disagrees with it to a greater or lesser extent. Just as the religion of Moses is background to all Jewish, Christian, and Muslim theology, the philosophy of the Upanishads underlies all Indian religion.

Upanishadic thought explains all existence in terms of one principle. This is the teaching that the only true or ultimate reality consists of eternal breath—*atman*—sometimes called

41

soul or spirit. In its cosmic form it is called the *Param-atman*, the breath which is "beyond" this sensory world. This Paramatman also is called the *Brahman-atman* (god-breath), or the World-soul. It is neither good nor evil, being beyond such distinctions. It is not personal, being called by a word which is neuter in gender. Out of this eternal principle emanates, in cyclical patterns, this world of time and space. But the so-called real world has actually only the appearance of reality; it is an apparent, temporary expression of the World-soul. This world is called *maya* (from the root *mā* "to measure"), a term which describes the nature of this world as limited by time and space, as opposed to true Paramatman, which is eternal and infinite. The maya world appears to be real only because of human ignorance, just as ignorance causes one to believe that a trick of magic produces a real result.

But in this maya world persons exist. The essential nature of a person, however, is not his maya body or his world of space and time. It is the fact that his body contains a portion of the World-soul, an atman which is a tiny part of the Paramatman. In some manner it has gotten caught in the cycles of time, and due to ignorance and past karma is being reborn again and again into this maya world. But this phenomenological world has no final or real existence and thus it has no positive value. The World-soul is all that truly is and all that matters. By the same token any notion that this present life is important—to think that maya existence is "real"—helps cause rebirth. Thus the basic meaning of life is found in knowing that one's own atman is truly part of the Paramatman. A famous illustration is found in the *Chāndogya Upanishad* where the father of the young man Shvetaketu is instructing him on the nature of the self and the true Self.

Place this salt in the water and come to me in the morning. Then he did so. Then he said to him, "That salt you placed in the water last evening, please bring it hither." Having looked for it he found it not, as it was completely dissolved.

"Please take a sip of it from this end." He said, "How is it?"

"Salt." "Take a sip from the middle. How is it?" "Salt." "Take a sip from the other end. How is it?" "Salt!" "Throw it away and come to me." He did so. It is always the same. Then he said to him, "Verily, indeed, my dear, you do not perceive Pure Being here. Verily, indeed, it is here."

That which is the subtle essence this whole world has for its self. That is the true. That is the self. That art thou, Shvetaketu.[16]

Since the deity, the Paramatman, is all and in all—since time and space are illusions of the mind—there is no doctrine of creation in Hinduism which is comparable to the story in Genesis. In the Upanishads the creator God of the early Vedic literature is held to be but a function of the World-soul, and in later Hinduism, the triad of gods who control the destiny of this maya world are themselves called "murtis," that is, congealings or condensations of the World-soul. Even the gods have no permanent, independent existence.

The "atheistic" heresy, Jainism. Jainism was founded about 500 B.C. by Vardhamana, who usually is referred to by the title Mahavira, which means "the great man." [17] In many ways his career and teachings parallel and resemble those of Gautama, the Buddha. Mahavira was of the Kshatriya, the nobility, or warrior class, which by the sixth century had been relegated to the second place by the Brahman, or priestly, class. In the main stream of Hindu teaching of that day it was believed that final release from rebirth was possible only for those of the highest class, so that by definition Mahavira was denied the possibility of ending the cycle of births at the end of his life. The best that he could hope for would be rebirth as a Brahman in his next life.

Although Mahavira accepted the notion of rebirth into this world by the influence of past karma, the Jain faith was heretical because its founder denied the authority of the Vedas and also opposed the orthodox class system. Instead of follow-

[16] VI:13:1-3. S. Radhakrishnan, The Principal Upaniṣads, (London: George Allen & Unwin, 1953), p. 463.
[17] See earlier discussion, chap. 1, p. 22.

ing the monism of the Upanishads, with the Paramatman, a maya world, and an individual atman for each person, Mahavira's position was much closer to the ancient Sankhya School (a dualistic philosophy which actually has survived to modern times). According to Mahavira's teaching there are two principles instead of one which account for existence. This world is not illusory, but real. In it are found two kinds of things, living and nonliving, which he called *jiva* and *ajiva*. The living jivas are souls, but they are not part of a World-soul for there is none such. There are millions of jivas, all immortal and of equal worth. In this free state they are blissful and all-knowing. Due to ignorance jivas become trapped in this world of things. Once a jiva becomes trapped in this world and enters a cycle of rebirths it may be reborn in any living form such as grass, man, cow, ant, or rat. At a level higher than this world there are gods who also are trapped in existence, but only for a time. They are in the same need of final release from the cycle of rebirths as is man but presently are living at a higher and more fortunate level.

This system has no room for a god or gods in the usual sense of the term, since no god can help man find release or gain the victory (*Jina*) over rebirth. Mahavira is reported to have called upon each person to work out his salvation with no hope of outside help. "Man! Thou art thy own friend; why wishest thou for a friend beyond thyself?" [18] His way of salvation involved a very strict asceticism, which called upon his followers to practice the most rigidly disciplined lives in order to avoid piling up karma which would weight one's jiva down and hold it to the cycle of rebirths.

*The way of the Buddha.* The other "atheistic" system of the sixth century B.C. is that founded by Gautama, the Buddha, or "the enlightened one" (567-487 B.C.). Like Mahavira, he also denied that there is a Paramatman. It appears that the Buddha also denied that man has a soul or atman which

[18] Hermann Jacobi, tr. *Gaina Sutras*, Sacred Books of the East (London: Oxford University Press, 1884), xxii, 33.

44

could be considered to be an emanation from a World-soul. But he did assume that man has an essential nature, a *purusha* or "stream of life" which is suffering through a cycle or series of existences. Like Mahavira, Gautama taught that every person determines his own destiny. Early tradition condensed his way of salvation into a succinct statement of Four Noble Truths concerning the nature of existence and the way to the cessation of rebirth. In the next chapter we will have occasion to discuss the nature of man, his plight and salvation in the teachings of the Buddha, but at this point we are concerned only with the question of the teaching about deity in Buddhism.

The Buddha taught that it is possible to stop one's cycle of rebirths by becoming enlightened—by knowledge of the cause of existence and the way to eliminate this cause. Each purusha must bring an end to his own cycle of lives by his own efforts, although he does have the assurance that where the Buddha has led others may follow. As inspiration he has the words of the Buddha concerning his own achievement of nirvana.

This is the Noble Truth concerning the Cessation of Suffering. Thus, monks, in things which formerly had not been heard have I obtained insight, knowledge, understanding, wisdom, intuition. . . .

And this knowledge and insight arose in my mind: The emancipation of my mind cannot be shaken; this is my last birth; now shall I not be born again.[19]

It is Buddhist tradition that the Buddha, prior to his enlightenment, had lived some of his earlier existences in the world of the gods without obtaining release from rebirth. His stress upon self-salvation reminds one of William Henley's cry of self-sufficiency:

[19] From the Mahāvagga of the Vinaya Texts. In E. H. Brewster, *Life of Gotama the Buddha.* Quoted in Clarence H. Hamilton, *Buddhism: A Religion of Infinite Compassion* (New York: The Bobbs-Merrill Company, 1952), p. 30.

> Out of the night that covers me,
>   Black as the Pit from pole to pole,
> I thank whatever gods may be
>   For my unconquerable soul.[20]

Thus it would appear that both Jainism and primitive Buddhism fall into a category which is at variance with biblical thought in that the only ultimate is the life, or life force, of the individual. There are no gods to serve, or to beseech for help. Instead each life must achieve for itself the cessation of rebirth into this world of suffering.

Although the Buddha himself probably taught that there is no god who can help man in his search for enlightenment and final release, a major movement of Buddhism does have a pantheon of savior gods. The Mahayana school of Buddhism arose in northwest India around the time of Christ. The unique contribution of this school of the "greater vehicle" is that of savior gods known as Bodhisattvas, "one whose essence is enlightened." Of obscure origin, perhaps influenced by Greek religions, perhaps influenced by the rise in Hinduism of the bhakti cult of Vishnu,[21] the Bodhisattva concept today is central to most of the Buddhism of China and Japan.

In Buddhist mythology a Bodhisattva is one who has broken the cycle of rebirths and achieved the right to enter nirvana, never again to be reborn into existence as we know it. But because of his love for humanity, and because of the compassion he feels for those who are still caught in the wheel of life, the Bodhisattva renounces entrance into nirvana and makes available to those who call upon him in prayer the tremendous amount of merit (good karma) which he has piled up for his own salvation. This savior-god tradition is predicated upon the compassionate vow of Gautama, the Buddha, to refuse to enter nirvana at the time of his own enlightenment, and upon the love he revealed in the forty-five years he devoted

[20] "Invictus."
[21] On the bhakti cults, see further pp. 73–76. Cf. Index.

to preaching the Norm to all who would listen. Thus we find that Buddhism, in its East Asian Mahayana form, is not to be labeled atheistic, even though it is probable that original Buddhism had no room for divine help on the road to salvation.

### Teachings About Deity in the Religions of China and Japan

Just as there is a common denominator to be found for the religions of biblical lands, as well as one for the religions of India, the religions of East Asia have in common the elements of nature worship and ancestor worship. In China there are two living religions which have survived from pre-Christian times. According to tradition, both Taoism and Confucianism arose in the sixth century B.C., but before these schools emerged there already existed a view of life which is referred to as early Sinaean (Chinese) religion. This included a cult of the ancestors, and also a reverence for the forces of nature symbolized by the concept of yang-yin. Yang is masculine, warm, and bright, while yin is feminine, damp, and dark. It was believed that the interaction of yang and yin accounted for the world of things and of men. At the same time it was believed that there was an underlying principle, the Tao, of which the yang and yin were but energy modes. In a general way it is helpful to think of Confucianism as stressing worship of the ancestors, and Taoism as stemming from and stressing the worship of nature.

Taoism. This is the name for the philosophy ascribed to the shadowy figure Lao Tzu (604-531 B.C.). It is not certain when or whether he lived, but Lao Tzu is given credit for the authorship of a book of poetry of some five thousand Chinese characters which is called the Tao Tê Ching. This brief book contains some eighty-one short poems on the subject of the meaning of the Tao. No names of persons or places occur in this writing, which consists essentially of a series of poetic explanations of the meaning of Tao, or the Way. This Way

47

would appear to be the way of the natural world and as such is something to be accepted and understood, rather than an abstraction to be explained. This Tao Tê, or natural way of virtue, is described variously. Thus in the first chapter we read:

> The Way that can be told of is not an Unvarying Way,
> The names that can be named are not unvarying names.
> It was from the Nameless that Heaven and Earth sprang;
> The named is but the mother that rears the ten thousand creatures, each after its kind.[22]

This underlying way of the natural world is to be followed for the happiest life, and any tampering with this way or any opposition to it is the cause of man's troubles. Chapter XIX says:

> Banish wisdom, discard knowledge,
> And the people will be benefited a hundredfold.
> Banish human kindness, discard morality,
> And the people will be dutiful and compassionate.
> Banish skill, discard profit,
> And thieves and robbers will disappear.[23]

This view of life can seem very simple, and even naïve, especially when presented in this brief form, but it represents a basic expression of man's understanding of the meaning of his existence, which is found also in Hinduism, in the Greek religious philosophy known as Stoicism, and in the Perennial Philosophy as described by Aldous Huxley. It essentially is a monism in that a single principle is used to explain all things. This principle can be grasped by intuition and mystical experience even though it does not lend itself to logical analysis.

[22] Arthur Waley, The Way and Its Power: A Study of the Tao Tê Ching and Its Place in Chinese Thought (Evergreen ed.; New York: Grove Press, 1958), p. 141. (London: George Allen and Unwin, 1934).
[23] Ibid., p. 166.

In Tao the only motion is returning;
The only useful quality, weakness.
For though all creatures under heaven
are the products of Being,
Being itself is the product of Not-being.[24]

Whatever the origins and actual meaning of the Tao Tê Ching, its philosophy was given dynamic expression by the writings of Chuang Tzu, who was active in the fourth century B.C. He has been called the "St. Paul" of Taoism, and by story, parable, and symbolic acts he sought to interpret the central message of the book of Tao for his day. Two quotations from the book of Chuang Tzu will help us understand his message.

When Chuang Tzu's wife died, Hui Tzu went to condole. He found the widower sitting on the ground, singing, with his legs spread out at a right angle, and beating time on a bowl.

"To live with your wife," exclaimed Hui Tzu, "and see your eldest son grow up to be a man, and then not to shed a tear over her corpse,—this would be bad enough. But to drum on a bowl, and sing; surely this is going too far."

"Not at all," replied Chuang Tzu. "When she died, I could not help being affected by her death. Soon, however, I remembered that she had already existed in a previous state before birth, without form, or even substance; that while in that unconditioned condition, substance was added to spirit; that this substance then assumed form; and that the next stage was birth. And now, by virtue of a further change, she is dead, passing from one phase to another like the sequence of spring, summer, autumn, and winter. And while she is thus lying asleep in Eternity, for me to go about weeping and wailing would be to proclaim myself ignorant of these natural laws. Therefore I refrain." [25]

We gain an even clearer insight into the monistic nature of Taoism by the following description of the dream and the dreamer:

[24] *Ibid.*, chap. XL, p. 192.
[25] *Chuang Tzu: Taoist Philosopher and Chinese Mystic*, tr. from the Chinese by Herbert Giles (Rev. ed.; London: George Allen & Unwin, 1926), p. 174.

Once upon a time, I, Chuang Tzu, dreamt I was a butterfly, fluttering hither and thither, to all intents and purposes a butterfly. I was conscious only of following my fancies as a butterfly, and was unconscious of my individuality as a man. Suddenly, I awaked, and there I lay, myself again. Now I do not know whether I was then a man dreaming I was a butterfly, or whether I am now a butterfly dreaming I am a man.[26]

If we ask, then, what Taoism teaches about the nature of deity, and of the relation of a god to this world, we find it expressed in the idea of the natural Way, a single, monistic principle. The Tao is not personal and is not creator of the universe so much as it is a principle which is inherent in all things, a natural way to be followed by anyone with the proper insight.

> Without leaving his door
> He knows everything under heaven.
> Without looking out of his window
> He knows all the ways of heaven.
> For the further one travels
> The less one knows.
> Therefore the Sage arrives without going,
> Sees all without looking,
> Does nothing, yet achieves everything.[27]

We are told, however, that the practical Chinese never turned to this philosophy in any real numbers for religious satisfaction. After Buddhism entered China, about the beginning of the Christian era, Taoism as a folk religion tended to degenerate into magical efforts to control the world of nature, but the influence of philosophical Taoism has continued with varying fortune right into the communistic era of Red China.[28]

---

[26] *Ibid.*, p. 47.

[27] Waley, *The Way and Its Power*, chap. XLVII, p. 200.

[28] Cf., e.g., Holmes Welch, *The Parting of the Way, Lao Tzu and the Taoist Movement* (Boston: Beacon Press, 1957); Lin Yutang, ed. and tr. *The Wisdom of Laotse* (New York: The Modern Library, 1948), pp. 15-21; Werner Eichhorn, "Taoism," in *The Concise Encyclopedia of Living Faiths*, R. C. Zaehner, ed. (New York: Hawthorn Books, 1959), p. 401.

*Confucianism.* The other basic expression of the meaning of life indigenous to China is found in the system of moral and political thought begun by Confucius (551-479 B.C.). He lived in a feudal age before the development of a true empire, but the school of thought which later took his name has been of prime importance in molding Chinese thought and action. We shall have occasion to discuss Confucius at greater length in chapter six, so that here we will be concerned only with his thinking on the subject of deity and the nature of the world.

Confucius apparently had a more personal conception of the meaning of Tao than is to be found in the religion of Taoism, and two terms which sometimes are translated into English by the word "God" appear in the *Analects*. The first, *shang-ti*, means something like "exalted ancestor," but appears only once. The second term, *t'ien*, means sky or heaven, and this term occurs fairly frequently and is used in a more personal way than shang-ti. Thus, in the Analects, VII:22, we read: "The Master said, Heaven begat the power (*tê*) that is in me. What have I to fear from such a one as Huan T'ui?" [29]

In a wider sense, however, we look in vain for the kind of presupposition or doctrine of a creator god who reveals his will to his chosen people that is found in the Bible. Confucius' context is quite different. He reflects the ancient Chinese view which taught that this world and its inhabitants are a result of the creative actions of the mysterious and unknowable Tao. Tao has set in motion the yang and yin, the male and female creative forces from whose actions all created things proceed. It was not, however, so much to follow the "way of heaven" to which he called men, but to the way of the ancients, which he assumed to be the best way for men to live. This way should be recovered and followed as a model for living. Yet this way of the ancients carried with it an uncritical acceptance of belief in the age-old polytheism and ancestor worship of China. In fact it seems probable that what little emphasis he

[29] *The Analects of Confucius*, Arthur Waley, tr. (Vintage Book; New York: Random House, 1938; London: George Allen and Unwin, 1938).

gave to worship of spirits and ancestors was based on his conviction that such worship was necessary to preserve the virtue of the people and the welfare of the state.

Someone asked for an explanation of the Ancestral Sacrifice. The Master said, I do not know. Anyone who knew the explanation could deal with all things under Heaven as easily as I lay this here; and he laid his finger upon the palm of his hand.

Of the saying, "The word 'sacrifice' is like the word 'present'; one should sacrifice to a spirit as though that spirit was present," the Master said, If I am not present at the sacrifice, it is as though there were no sacrifice.[30]

Although Confucius has been called an agnostic and also a humanist, it would appear that we do not have sufficient materials reflecting Confucius' thought on the question of deity to come to any conclusions on this matter.

In chapter one we noted that the Japanese concept of *kami* (supernatural power), as employed in the myths of the Shinto scripture, the *Ko-ji-ki*, is used to designate the Japanese Islands, the people, and the forces of nature. Although in modern times pure Shinto no longer exists because it has been modified under the strong influences of Chinese and Buddhist thought, the concept of deity in Shinto would appear to involve a polytheistic combination of nature and ancestor worship. Such nature deities as the sun goddess, Amaterasu, and the storm god, Susa-no-wo, are important, and before the end of World War II the emperor himself was considered to be divine;[31] however, there is lacking a single creator deity, such as is found in the religions of biblical lands, or a monistic source of all existence, as in Hinduism. Instead we have a polytheism which is clearly indicated in the Japanese name for their religion, *kami no michi*, "the way of the gods."

[30] *Ibid.*, III:11-12.
[31] Since the renunciation of divinity by the emperor of Japan was ordered by the victorious Western allies this does not preclude such belief on the part of the Japanese people.

## The Concept of Deity in the World's Religions

Let us now summarize what we have stated to be the teaching about the nature of deity in the major religions. The monotheistic religions, Judaism, Christianity, and Islam, proclaim a creator God, who has made the world, wherein each person is a unique creation. In India the pattern is quite different. The main stream of philosophical Hinduism is basically monistic, meaning that one single principle, the World-soul, or Paramatman, accounts for all that truly is. Man is reborn into a maya, or illusory world, and his true goal is to link his atman once again with the Paramatman whence it came. Although god is in man, god is not the creator of man nor of the world, even though the world might be considered to be an emanation from god.

Buddhism and Jainism, the two heresies which broke with Hinduism, are dualistic in principle. In these religions the present world is considered to be real and is labeled evil rather than illusory, while each living being represents a life principle trapped in existence. But in these two religions (at least in their earliest forms) we look in vain for the teaching of a god who can help man in his search for release from the cycle of rebirths. Instead each person must save himself by his own unaided effort. And finally, in the religions native to China and Japan, although we find that the world is considered to be real and good, there is no teaching of a creator god. Instead we find nature and ancestor worship, with man's duty to the world of the supernatural requiring propitiation of the gods of nature and of the departed ancestors.

There would appear, therefore, to be no principle of deity which is common to all of the world's religions. Instead man's religions fall into patterns which we have called circles of faith. Within each circle of faith is found a basic teaching about the nature of deity and the world. And where one circle of faith teaches that each man is created by god, another affirms that he is reborn into the world. Where one circle of

53

faith teaches that man must rely upon his god for his salvation, another teaches that man must save himself.

Who then is God? At the beginning of the chapter, reference was made to Aldous Huxley's book, *The Perennial Philosophy*. The thesis of his study is that all religions are at base the same, since all rest upon a Ground of Being, which is the ultimate reality experienced by all religious men everywhere. What Huxley actually has done is to assume a position very close to Hindu Vedanta and insist that this monism is the only true position. In other words he has taken one circle of faith and claimed to find that all other religions coincide with this Hindu position. In Huxley's words:

Our starting point has been the psychological doctrine, "That art thou." The question that now quite naturally presents itself is a metaphysical one: What is the That to which the thou can discover itself to be akin?

To this the fully developed Perennial Philosophy has at all times and in all places given fundamentally the same answer. The divine Ground of all existence is a spiritual Absolute, ineffable in terms of discursive thought, but (in certain circumstances) susceptible of being directly experienced and realized by the human being. This Absolute is the God-without-form of Hindu and Christian mystical phraseology. . . . Out of any given generation of men and women very few will achieve the final end of human existence; but the opportunity for coming to unitive knowledge will, in one way or another, continually be offered until all sentient beings realize Who in fact they are.[32]

These sentiments can be paralleled by quotations from the Hindu philosopher S. Radhakrishnan, for instance, or from almost any writer on Hindu Vedanta. But they also can be clearly and categorically denied by quotations from Christian theologians. Huxley states again and again that he is explaining Vedanta. The only question is, does his analysis fit any other circle of faith such as that of Judaism, or of Islam, Shinto, or Jainism? Huxley claimed for all religions the common de-

[32] P. 21.

nominator of a monistic metaphysic in which the goal of life is to recognize that the individual self is but an aspect of the Ground of Being. Although certain passages of Christian literature, especially from the mystics, can be shown to have affinity with Huxley's interpretation of the Ground of Being, this fact is capable of other explanations than the one he suggests.[33] But, as has frequently been pointed out, whereas in Vedantic thought its god *becomes* the world, for the Bible its god *creates* the world and all that it contains, and there is a world of difference between these two positions.

Surprisingly, this same error in reverse has been made in the past by Christian missionaries. These Christian apologists often have announced that followers of other religions, in their ignorance, actually are serving the true God of the Bible. Hindus, e.g., were told that they have the truth only partially revealed to them, but that they will find the whole truth when they turn to the God of the Bible. In our day Hindus are telling Christians that the god of the Bible, as creator and guide of history, is but a lesser deity (comparable to the Hindu god, Brahma, or perhaps Vishnu), and they add that although it is all right to serve Yahweh, he is properly to be regarded as but a lower form of the World-soul. They maintain that only when Christians turn to Hinduism and its teaching of the Paramatman will they find the true meaning of existence.[34] In other words, the earlier error of some Christian missionary apologists has come back to their children with double force. Would it not be better if both the Christian and the Hindu were to accept the position that the nameless god of Huxley, or the god with a thousand names of Hinduism, is not the same as the god of Moses and Jesus?

In chapter eight we will discuss the question of tolerance,

[33] Cf., e.g., R. C. Zaehner, *Mysticism, Sacred and Profane: An Inquiry into Some Varieties of Praeternatural Experiences* (New York: Oxford University Press, 1957). Cf. also I Cor. 12:1-3.

[34] Cf. Swami Prabhavananda (with the assistance of Frederick Manchester), *The Spiritual Heritage of India* (New York: Doubleday & Company, 1963). In this book the Swami claims that the Vedanta is the essence of all true religion.

but in relation to the question of "Who God is," if we are to think clearly, we must beware of such labels as "tolerant" or "intolerant." Would it not be better to realize that any position affirmed by man is set in a circle of faith? The Christian, though he can proclaim it as a fact, cannot prove that his God exists. Aldous Huxley stated that his Ground of Being is "ineffable in terms of discursive thought," though he was convinced of its reality. The Hindu cannot prove the existence of the Paramatman nor the "fact" of rebirth, though these are basic to his world view. Each is affirming his own presuppositions and therefore neither is more nor less intolerant than the other. The biblical position, that there is only one true God, is just as valid as any other, and the Christian is not bigoted merely because he affirms it. So, too, the Hindu is not necessarily more "spiritual" because he affirms this world to be maya. This is his circle of faith.

Yet if it is a fact that all religions are true, there is, for instance, no point to Christianity, nor, for that matter, to any religion. Or, to paraphrase the apostle Paul, "If salvation were possible through Judaism, then Christ died to no purpose." [35] And as a Christian one must insist that God does have a name. To call God the nameless does indeed fit a monism where god is neither male nor female and has a thousand names—or no name. But biblical religion affirms that the creator God has revealed his purpose to his creatures in history. And in history man must make a choice. In the words of Joshua: "Choose this day whom you will serve, whether the gods your fathers served in the region beyond the River, or the gods of the Amorites in whose land you dwell; but as for me and my house, we will serve [Yahweh]." [36]

[35] Gal. 2:21. "For if justification were through the law, then Christ died to no purpose."
[36] Josh. 24:15.

CHAPTER 3

# WRETCHED MAN
# THAT I AM!

Search as they will, anthropologists have been unable to discover a human society without religion. It has been suggested that the essential difference between man and "the other animals" is that man, alone of all living beings, is religious. Although religion is a complex subject, it is still possible to reduce the nature of all religions to one common denominator—religion always involves man's search for security in a world that appears to be hostile to his own interests. In other words, from the point of view of the anthropologist —the scientist who studies man as man—the story of religion is the story of man's search for salvation, of his various attempts to find meaning in life and to live with hope rather than fear.

It is axiomatic for all religions that man is in need of help in a world which is dangerous and unfriendly. Anyone who has eyes to see soon learns that "man is born to die"; that hurricane, flood, famine, disease, and warfare stalk the earth; and that fear, greed, anger, and hate dominate the lives of men and the affairs of society. The question "What must I do to be saved?" lies at the center of the teaching of each religion. Yet this question often is misunderstood, especially in our Western culture. This misunderstanding usually takes the form of a mistaken emphasis in thinking and teaching about salvation as having to do essentially only with life after death, with the ultimate destiny of man. On the contrary, although salvation as taught in any one religion might include beliefs about man's fate after death, the real meaning of the word concerns, first of all, one's present condition in relation to the forces and situations which influence one's life.

The Latin word *salutas* means "to be healthy" and survives today, not only in the word "salvation," but also in the word "salute," or in the toast of health such as the Spanish *saludas*. In most religions the phrase "to be saved" describes one's condition in relation to the spiritual forces which control the affairs of men. Is one's relationship to the gods such that they will save him from disaster and bring him good fortune or health? What religious beliefs and practices can bring salvation so that fear is replaced with hope, disease with health, and death with life?

In chapters six and seven of Paul's Letter to the Romans he deplores his helpless condition in the face of the many temptations and satanic forces which appeared ready to engulf him. This complaint culminates in his famous cry of despair, "Wretched man that I am! Who will deliver me from this body of death?" [1] The positive statement of Paul which appears at the end of the eighth chapter illustrates the meaning of salvation with which we are concerned:

Who shall separate us from the love of Christ? Shall tribulation, or distress, or persecution, or famine, or nakedness, or peril, or sword? . . . No, in all these things we are more than conquerors through him who loved us. For I am sure that neither death, nor life, nor angels, nor principalities, nor things present, nor things to come, nor powers, nor height, nor depth, nor anything else in

[1] Rom. 7:24.

all creation, will be able to separate us from the love of God in Christ Jesus our Lord.[2]

Salvation means to be saved *from* unwanted situations and conditions and to be saved *to* desirable living. How widespread is the desire for security and hope and the opportunity to live the fullest life possible! In the secular world the search for "salvation" is evident on every hand. The political platforms of the major parties offer security from unemployment and from fear of old age, and they promise leadership toward world peace. We continually are asked to lend support to proposals to meet the burgeoning need of psychiatric help for a generation of frightened persons with a high rate of alcoholism, divorce, and violence. It is unfortunate that the phrase "to be saved" has lost its value and meaning for many simply because it has been misused by some of the Christian holiness groups. The concept is so central to any religion that one must understand its meaning for that religion before it is possible to see clearly what constitutes the appeal of that religion to its followers.

To use an illustration from the world of politics and economics, we find that Marxist communism teaches that religion is "an opiate for the masses," and that it is utilized by the bourgeoisie to lull the proletariat into meek submission by the promise of "pie in the sky when you die." By making use of the mistaken notion that salvation has to do only with life after death, and by its teaching of atheism, thereby denying a world of the supernatural, communism claims to lead man beyond the "superstitions" of religion to a materialism which frees man from the chains of the church and from a false faith in a God who is dead. The irony of this is that *The Communist Manifesto* simply substitutes a new kind of salvation for the one which it attacks. "Man's present plight," says the Marxist, "stems from his failure to solve the economic problems which have arisen in capitalistic society." Man is regarded as an "economic animal" and, if the world could only accept

[2] Vss. 35-36, 38-39.

the communistic analysis and solution to man's economic problems, a utopian age of peace, prosperity, and security for all would follow. Marxist salvation differs from the Christian religion in claiming man to be an "economic animal" rather than a child of God. It also denies the existence of any supernatural powers which might come to the aid of man. Yet the "dialectic of history" which is basic to Marxist theory is substituted for the old supernaturalism, and the inexorable nature of its relentless progress toward a classless society is referred to frequently as a sanction to gain acceptance for this creed.

## Man's Plight and Salvation in Various Religions

This chapter deals with two problems related to the nature of man and his salvation. The first question concerns the doctrine of man and the nature of the plight in which he finds himself according to primitive religion, the biblical tradition (the Jew, Christian, and Muslim), Hinduism, Buddhism, and Confucianism. The second problem concerns what each of these religions teaches about salvation—about the way in which man may find meaning, help, and security in this present life. The purpose of this comparison is to continue the development of our thesis of "circles of faith." This thesis assumes that each religion begins with its own presuppositions and to that extent is unique in its teachings on any basic theme of religion, such as salvation. It also assumes that each religion affirms its peculiar message on the basis of its own unproved presuppositions.

*Salvation in primitive religion.* Although there actually is no such thing as "primitive religion" as an entity which exists in time and space, scholars are in wide agreement upon what constitutes religion from the point of view of primitive or uncivilized man. It is a bit dangerous to begin a discussion of "sin and salvation" with primitive religion, because this world view can so easily be tagged with a label such as "superstitious," "unscientific," or "prerational." For many this is the same thing as saying it is not worth bothering with, at least insofar as it might have any relevance for sophisticated, modern man. This is unfortunate, because it is precisely in this area of primitive religion that man can learn much about himself, his fears, hopes, and deep-rooted anxieties about the meaning of his life.[3] It has been suggested that primitive religion is to be found in at least four places in the experience of man as a race: back in time before recorded history; in the backwaters or out-of-the-way places of the world, such as Central Africa or the Amazon Valley; at the low level of all religions (including Christianity); and finally, deep down inside each of us. To ask what sin and salvation mean to the primitive, therefore, might tell us much about what these terms should mean to us.

Primitive man's world is best described as emotional rather than rational. He might be said to feel his world rather than to think about it. There is an aliveness which characterizes his world which survives in our language in many words and phrases. For instance, we ascribe personality to such inanimate objects as an automobile, especially an old jalopy, or a chair over which we happen to stumble in the dark. We describe a coronary thrombosis as a heart "attack," a brain hemorrhage as a "stroke," implying that some supernatural force has "seized" a person. To a far greater degree than such terms suggest, the primitive feels that the world in which he lives is alive with dangerous power which might at any time break forth upon him.

The scholarly term for this undifferentiated force is mana, a word taken from the southern Pacific islands of Melanesia. This mana refers to the concept of supernatural force which is thought to be all around and in everything. It is mana which makes the sun hot, which makes the crops sprout, which causes growth and decay. The stronger and braver warrior has more mana than the one less "endowed," while a terrify-

[3] Cf., e.g., Mircea Eliade, The Sacred and the Profane: The Nature of Religion, tr. from the French by Willard R. Trask (Torchbook ed.; New York: Harper & Row, 1961).

61

ing stroke of lightning, a smallpox plague, or a forest fire represents mana in action. An important characteristic of mana is that it is considered amoral, that is, neither good nor bad of itself. It is, rather, naked power which one must continually guard against lest it bring harm rather than good. It is something like electricity, not only in the mysterious nature of its potency, but also in that electricity also is amoral—it can cook one's dinner or electrocute a person without warning. There is no concept of cause and effect involved, but instead the primitive is concerned first of all with getting along with this power in such a way that it will do him the most good and the least harm.

In this primitive world man appears to think of himself as not much different from the animals, or even from the trees, streams, or other moving or living things. He is a man-animal who must get along in this world of strange forces as best he can. This man-animal has a charge of mana in him which gives him strength and life. If this force leaves his body death will ensue. In the simple primitive society there is seldom any concept of a creator god, of a soul as such, or even of a life after death.[4] Salvation, therefore, to the primitive involves three things: (1) retaining his mana force; (2) knowing the methods and having the tools to cause mana to work for him and benefit him; (3) preventing mana from doing anything that is not desired.

Typical beliefs and practices of the primitive are actually aspects of primitive man's way of finding security in relation to this naked force of mana. Thus a graveyard contains mana potency of the spirits of the dead, and so it is *tabu*. It is a "forbidden" place except under carefully controlled conditions which will neutralize the ability of the mana to harm members of the tribe. It might be tabu to eat a certain food before a hunt lest this act drain off the mana of the hunters and lead

---

[4] Although there is no consensus on this statement, it would appear to hold for at least the most primitive of societies. For a recent summary of the question of the "High God" see Geoffrey Parrinder, *African Traditional Religion* (New York: Seabury Press, 1962), Chapter III, "The Supreme Being."

to failure. Again, a *fetish* contains mana power available to aid its owner. This might be an amulet, or perhaps a "lucky" spear which always has sufficient mana power to hit its target. The medicine man is one who knows the mysterious ways of mana and who possesses knowledge of the magical words and actions necessary to channel mana, either to his own advantage or, hopefully, in the tribe's interests. The whole world of the primitive is caught up in such notions. Man lives in a dangerous world, is enslaved to fear, and his salvation lies in learning the tabus and other means which the tribe has developed to get along with the potency of mana which is all around him.

*Salvation in Judaism, Christianity, and Islam.* Within any particular religion, or group of related religions, there is a certain inner consistency to be found between various doctrines, such as those about the nature of deity and of man. As was noted in chapter two, each of the three monotheistic religions which arose in the Near East—Judaism, Christianity, and Islam—holds that this world and its inhabitants are the result of the creative act of its God. Since man, therefore, is by nature a creature he ought to obey and serve God as the author and lord of his life. The famous phrase, "The chief end of man is to glorify God and to enjoy him forever," though Calvinist in origin, expresses this biblical view of man. The God of the Jew, Christian, and Muslim not only is creator, but he also is lord of history and the final arbiter of each man's destiny.

At the same time, although man ought to serve his creator, these religions assume that man has the freedom to choose either to obey his God or to follow his own desires. Volumes have been written about "the mystery of freedom," but the essential meaning of this doctrine is that it affirms that man can truly serve his God only when he is free to choose either to obey or disobey. Without freedom to choose, man's service to God would be but the actions of a puppet which has no will of its own. It is the mistaken use of this freedom, however, in man's selfish and willful disobedience of God's way, and the "sinful" following of his own way, which is blamed for most of the troubles that afflict biblical man. The myth of Adam and Eve, and of their sin in paradise, is a story of disobedience and willful action used, at least in part, to explain why man's life is so full of toil and trouble and why he must die. The stories of the flood and of the tower of Babel in the early chapters of Genesis also affirm that whenever man follows his own way the result is murder, warfare, and confusion. The ensuing history of the Israelites stresses that whenever the people are willful and rebellious they suffer persecution, enslavement, and other disasters. Only if they turn to God and his saving power will they find hope and help, and the stories of the Bible relate the miraculous nature of God's help which overcomes obstacles against which man by his unaided efforts would be helpless. Such events as the exodus from Egypt and the miraculous crossing of the Red Sea, the conquest of Palestine against apparently impossible odds, the vindication of the prophet Elijah on Mt. Carmel, and the return of the Jews from the Babylonian exile under the benign rule of the Persians are cited as proof that true salvation comes only from the God of the Jews.

In later centuries the Christians were to proclaim God's saving power as manifested in raising Jesus from the dead after selfish and willful men had put him to death. Still later the Muslims were to tell of the many ways in which Allah had revealed his salvation in the marvelous career of his prophet, Muhammad, who was supported by Allah even though at times it appeared as though the whole world was bent on destroying him.

Now if salvation lies in obeying and serving one's God, the crucial question becomes: "How can I know and do the will of God?" It is precisely here that Jew, Christian, and Muslim differ in their understanding of the form and content of God's revelation for the salvation of mankind. Thus early Judaism based its understanding of saving revelation on the covenant made between their God, Yahweh, and the Israelites when he saved them from Egyptian slavery. The classical expression of this covenant is found in the Law of Moses, known as the Torah, the first five books of the Bible. The Old Testament books of law and history testify further that if the people obey God's will as revealed in the Torah, if they serve him and do not serve any other god, all will be well with them; but if they disobey, disaster will result. This theme is found in every part of the Jewish scriptures. It is true that in the context of this covenant belief there was some disagreement over the true nature of Yahweh's demands on his chosen people. The priestly writers, as might be expected, stressed cultic and legal demands, the prophets emphasized that it was Yahweh's will that the people practice social justice and righteousness, and the wisdom teachers called for a return to civic and social virtues, but all were agreed on the priority of obedience and service to God as necessary for the well-being both of the individual and the nation.

In spite of the efforts of priest and prophet to lead the people to obedience to Yahweh, the Jews continued to be involved in many disasters. The division of the Hebrew kingdom after the death of Solomon, the destruction of the northern kingdom by the Assyrians, the destruction of Jerusalem and the Babylonian exile, domination by Persian, Greek, and Roman Empires, the Roman destruction of Jerusalem in A.D. 70, the loss of the homeland of Palestine, the heavy inroads made upon its numbers by Christian conversions, and finally the very proscription of Judaism by Constantine—all culminated in an emphasis upon rules and duties as the truest expression of God's demands upon his people. Although the prophetic stress on ethics and love and justice was never lost sight of, Judaism sought more and more to "build a fence around the Law" which would protect the Law from erosion and help protect the faithful who followed it from further disaster. The result was Rabbinic Judaism based on the Talmud, a compendium of teachings and rules, completed about A.D. 500. Its purpose is to enable the orthodox Jew to know the will of God for every circumstance and thus to make clear the way of salvation. To this day the traditional Jew seeks his

65

salvation by following its teachings, for he thereby can learn how to serve and please God and receive his approval and blessing. In spite, therefore, of the Roman dispersion of the Jews and the end of the Jewish nation as an entity, communities of Jews continued, through the centuries, to flourish in a world which is ignorant of the Torah and often hostile to those who would follow its teachings.

Christianity, which arose out of Judaism, places the locus of revelation in the life, death, and resurrection of Jesus, whom it claims as the Jewish Messiah or Christ. It agrees with Judaism in tracing the cause of man's present plight to rebellion, the living of one's life apart from God. Jesus' proclamation of the imminence of God's rule or kingdom was a summons for men to turn from their sinful and selfish ways to obedience and service to God. The apostle Paul also called upon men to turn to God for their salvation, and to turn from the worship of idols and from following their own selfish ways. The proof for Paul that God can save man from bondage even to such supernatural forces as sin, the devil, and death was found by him in the power that God displayed in raising Jesus from the dead, and in making the power of the Holy Spirit available to those who turned to God in faith. By the power of the Holy Spirit, claimed Paul, one could live a Christ-centered life of obedience to God rather than a self-centered life of meaninglessness and fear. In his letter to the Christians in the churches of Galatia (in Asia Minor) Paul contrasts his view of a selfish life with one lived in obedience to God with the help of the Holy Spirit.

But I say, walk by the Spirit, and do not gratify the desires of the flesh. For the desires of the flesh are against the Spirit, and the desires of the Spirit are against the flesh; for these are opposed to each other, to prevent you from doing what you would. But if you are led by the Spirit you are not under the law. Now the works of the flesh are plain: immorality, impurity, licentiousness, idolatry, sorcery, enmity, strife, jealousy, anger, selfishness, dissension, party spirit, envy, drunkenness, carousing, and the like. I warn you, as

I warned you before, that those who do such things shall not inherit the kingdom of God. But the fruit of the Spirit is love, joy, peace, patience, kindness, goodness, faithfulness, gentleness, self-control; against such there is no law. And those who belong to Christ Jesus have crucified the flesh with its passions and desires.[5]

It would appear that Paul here is drawing a sharp distinction between the self-centered way of the disobedient world of men and the ideal way of salvation for the Christian, who, since he has submitted himself to God's rule (kingdom) by faith in Christ, should live a Christ-centered life. It is true that Paul addressed the above words to Christians who were quarreling among themselves, but he proclaimed that the Christian must turn from the ways of man to the way of God, who alone is worthy to be obeyed, and who alone has power to save man from his selfish nature. It was for Paul a fact that disobedient and sinful men had crucified Jesus, but that God had once again proven his power to save by raising Jesus from the dead and making him Messiah, or Christ, the one through whom God's salvation for all mankind had been revealed. Just as the Jew follows God's will through the Torah, the Christian must follow God as revealed in Christ if he would escape the chaos, meaninglessness, and oblivion of the way of the world.

Finally, although the Muslims accept Moses and Jesus as two of the twenty-eight genuine prophets of Allah, they hold that Allah's final revelation of his way of salvation for all the world was revealed through the Seal of the prophets, Muhammad, the Messenger of Allah. This revelation, which supersedes all previous revelations, is contained in the Qur'an, the "reciting" by Muhammad of Allah's message. The Qur'an, therefore, also supersedes both the Jewish and the Christian scriptures, although they are believed to be divinely inspired. If the Muslim seeks to serve Allah according to the revelation contained in the Qur'an he will find true peace and salvation which results from submission (Islam) to the will of Allah.

[5] Gal. 5:16-24.

Islam, like Judaism and Christianity, is a highly ethical religion which enjoins the faithful to live exemplary lives which will reflect Allah's loving care for them. The straight path of submission is also clearly indicated in the five doctrines which each Muslim must accept, and in the five duties which each must seek to fulfill. The five doctrines of the creed of Islam—the doctrines concerning Allah, his angels, his books, his prophets, and the final day of judgment—emphasize the central doctrine of the sovereignty of Allah and of the benefits of submission to his will. The five duties, known as the Five Pillars of the Faith, which each Muslim willingly performs within the limits of his ability, demonstrate one's willing submission to Allah's will and also give concrete expression to one's support of the brotherhood of the faithful, the Muslim community. These duties are public confession (stating at least once, publicly and with sincerity, the *Kalima:* "There is no God except Allah, and Muhammad is the Messenger of Allah"), public prayer, almsgiving, fasting, and daily prayers toward Mecca. Those who are converted to Islam, and thereby submit to Allah's sovereignty, enter the *dar al-Islam,* the household of Islam. Those outside the faith dwell in *dar al-harb,* the house of the enemy. Only the Muslim can experience the peace and meaning which are to be found in submission to Allah's will. As is true for the Jew and the Christian, those who do not accept the true way of salvation are cut off from salvation and live in a world which is perishing. The prayerful words of the first Sura or chapter of the Qur'an, recited almost daily by most Muslims states:

> In the name of Allah, the Merciful, the Compassionate.
> Praise be to Allah, Lord of mankind,
> The Merciful, the Compassionate,
> Master of the Day of Judgment.
> Thee do we worship, and to Thee do we turn for help.

Guide us in the straight path,
The path of those to whom Thou hast been gracious,
Not that of those with whom Thou art angered,
    nor of those who go astray.[6]

*Salvation in Hinduism.* As we have already noted, Hinduism is an extremely complex religion. But in terms of man's plight —the bondage under which he lives—it is possible to be fairly explicit without undue distortion. The monism of the Upanishads (Hindu scriptures of about 600 B.C.) described in chapter two[7] involves a doctrine of man and of this present world which has proved to be the classic expression of Indian religious thought. All later theology either develops the position, as does Vedanta; breaks with it, as did Jainism and Buddhism; or modifies in various ways its view of the world and of ways of release open to those trapped in the existence of this time-bound world.

Since for this classical monism the ultimate reality is the Paramatman, the World-soul or breath which is beyond (*para*) this world of time and physical existence, all that appears to us in this present world is termed maya, limited or illusory. Man is made up of an atman, breath, and also a maya body.[8] Ignorance causes him to think of this present world as both real and important. Man is *reborn* from his previous life into this maya world because of ignorance and past karma, and his present birth is predetermined by the amount and quality of this past karma. Although life in this world might be most happy and satisfying to a Hindu, his true destiny and real meaning are to be found in the solution of one problem—of how to bring to an end the cycle of rebirths in which his atman is involved.

Salvation as a general term in religion, we have said, con-

---

[6] Jeffery, *Islam*, p. 86.
[7] See above, pp. 41–43.
[8] For an analysis of the composition of man in Hindu thought see Franklin Edgerton, *The Bhagavad Gītā, Part 2: Interpretation and Arnold's Translation*, Harvard Oriental Series, XXXIX (Cambridge: Harvard University Press, 1944), 37-43.

cerns first of all this present life, with the goal of achieving security and meaning in this world. This is true even though the desired salvation might be closely linked with one's final destiny. What then does the Hindu believe about this present life, about what he must do to feel secure and to live with hope, so that he will have the fullest possible earthly existence? Traditionally there are three roads the Hindu can travel, three *margas* (paths) to follow. To a certain extent the first path is involved in the second and third, and some follow all three at the same time since they actually are three ways to the same goal.

The first of these is called *karma-marga*, or the way of deeds. It has been compared to the teaching of the New Testament Letter of James in that the stress is upon right living or good works. According to the level of one's birth into the hereditary class system, each person has a *dharma*, or duty, to fulfill. This duty is contained for some in the ancient *Laws of Manu* (c. the time of Christ) wherein the proper thoughts and actions which will ensure the production of good karma are presented in detail. It is believed that by following this guide rigorously one can live happily in this life and at the same time guarantee a better rebirth in the next stage of the continuing cycle of rebirths. In this scheme the cycle is endless until or unless one is reborn into the highest class, that of the Brahman, or priestly, class. Only those so reborn can hope for union of one's atman with the Paramatman at death, when the cycle is brought to an end and peace is found at last. It is easy to see why the Brahman class teaches this belief and also why this form of Hinduism often is called Brahmanism. Even when one chooses to follow either of the other two ways of life, the basic ethical and ritualistic teachings and practices of *karma-marga* are followed, with some modification.

Since the final cessation of rebirths for those who follow the karma-marga is restricted by definition to the priestly class, a second way of salvation is followed by some. This is called *jnana-marga*, or the way of knowledge. This way also is ancient, being found in the Upanishads at least as early as 500 B.C. Since the knowledge involved is esoteric and cannot be taught without much preparation on the part of the seeker, and then only after much mental and spiritual discipline, this way can be described but not explained. Along with the presupposition that one's atman is reborn into this world because of past karma goes the teaching that the whole cycle was begun originally by a kind of ignorance. If this ignorance can be replaced by the right kind of knowledge, continued rebirth can be brought to an end.

What is it that binds man to the wheel of existence? What are the chains from which he could free himself if only he knew the way? It is the mistaken notion—the delusion—that this present world is important in any real sense of the term. Most of us, instead of recognizing this world as maya, as transitory, think and act as though it were of real value. We think of self and of others as real persons and attach importance to such things as station in life, economic security, and possession of a wife and children; we mistakenly seek happiness in the simple pleasures of life. In a word, we think that what we do in this life has real meaning and that it is important to be an accepted part of society. This delusion causes us to act in such a way that we continue to forge bonds which chain us to the cycle of existence. By having emotions of love, hate, fear, anger, and greed we pile up karma which causes rebirth. By marriage and by struggle for position we do the same. This is all mistaken.

It might be interesting to quote here the words of a Western philosopher, Epictetus the Stoic (c. A.D. 50-135), whose analysis of the nature and meaning of life may well have been influenced by Indian thought. It was the Stoic view that unhappiness and evil in the lives of men resulted from desire and fear. Zeno (the founder of Stoicism) taught men a value that would be secure from the whims of chance, and from fear of exile, slavery, death, or any other external event which might rob man of his happiness. His message was that "a man is happy when what he wills exists." That is, man is to fit his life

71

into harmony with all that transpires, whatever it may be, in such a way that he has no concern—no fear or desire—about what happens. To live according to nature means that one should have no attached feelings toward any of the externals of life. Epictetus gave expression to this in such statements as the following:

One man is not unfortunate because of another.[9]

Why, then, are we angry? Because we admire the goods of which these men rob us. For, mark you, stop admiring your clothes, and you are not angry at the man who steals them; stop admiring your wife's beauty, and you are not angry at her adulterer.[10]

For the Hindu who is following the way of knowledge, of jnana-marga, to attach any lasting value to this present world is to show oneself to be ignorant of the true nature of self—mistakenly to treat this maya world as though it had permanent and abiding value. On the other hand, the one who attains to salvation is the one who experiences the final truth of life which is expressed in a famous and simple phrase, *tat tvam asi*. This Sanskrit phrase is easy to translate for Westerners simply because it contains words for which we have direct parallels in such cognate languages as English, French, and German. The word *tat* is close to the English word "that"; *tvam* (tuam) is close to "thou"; and the word *asi* is the second person singular form of the verb "to be," meaning "art" or "are." But what does "that thou art" mean? This phrase expresses the recognition that if one cuts through the deluding mists of this maya world and is granted a glimpse of the ultimate which lies beyond space and time—of the World-soul or Paramatman—he can experience the bliss of nirvana, of extinction of the self (even if but for a moment) while still in this life. It is the knowledge that the true self is that portion of the Paramatman which resides in one as his atman.

[9] *Epictetus*, tr. by W. A. Oldfather, The Leob Classical Library (Cambridge: Harvard University Press, 1925), I.ix.34.
[10] *Ibid.*, I.xviii.11.

It is the realization that one's maya body and this maya world are illusory. It is the end of the mistaken notion that one is an individual: One's apparent selfhood is lost by being merged into the ocean of being. But this apparent loss brings peace and bliss to replace the confusions and anxieties which characterize the lives of those who mistake existence in this world for true reality.

In order to approach this experience of the inflooding knowledge of "who I really am," it became customary in ancient times to renounce all ties with the world. This involved leaving wife, children, and livelihood in order to seek the knowledge which alone frees one from the cycle of births. This radical rejection of the world has been normative for the holy man throughout subsequent Indian history, although it is now being challenged on practical grounds by policies of the Indian government. It is obvious, however, that this way could not be followed by even a bare majority without a complete breakdown of society, including the impoverishment of those who feed the wandering ascetics. History records that although most Hindus might admire and envy those who have left all material possessions to save their own souls, this way has not proved popular to most. The ties of life have proved to be stronger than the fears of rebirth.

It is for this great majority that the third way of salvation is offered in Hinduism. This is *bhakti-marga*, the way of devotion (loving attachment) to a savior god. At least 300 million followers are claimed for the two major Hindu sects which offer salvation by faith in such a god. Bhakti-marga teaches, in principle, that there is divine help available to man in his attempts to find meaning in life and to realize his true destiny. As we have seen, the way of knowledge requires discipline and meditation of a most demanding sort. Such salvation by knowledge of the Paramatman is difficult to experience. But it is popularly believed that lesser aspects of the World-soul, emanations from the eternal ground of being, exist in the form of three manifestations of the World-soul. Of these three the first is Brahma, the creator god, and receives but

73

little attention from devotees. Perhaps this is because the whole idea of creation, which Brahma represents, involves the concepts of maya and rebirth which lie at the root of man's problems.

The two main gods of the bhakti cults are Vishnu and Shiva, and the cultic practices of the sects vary greatly. Each of these, however, makes available saving power for the believer and offers thereby salvation to any who will trust in him and turn to him for help. Vishnu is worshiped primarily through his *avatars*, or earthly manifestations, while Shiva is worshiped through his *shakti* (male energy) power, as mediated through his female consorts, such as Kali or Durga. For our purposes we can consider these two sects together because each offers divine help for problems in this life, and, for those devoted to the deity, the hope of cessation of rebirth at death.

Vishnu comes to the aid of mankind whenever the evil in the world threatens to overbalance the good. His most popular manifestation is as Krishna, whose legendary life is surrounded with myths of his victories over evil and the limitations of this maya world. The *Bhagavad-gita*, "The Song of the Beloved One," is the most famous scripture of the followers of Vishnu. In this poem Krishna's message is that if one turns to Vishnu with trusting devotion (bhakti) and places all his reliance upon the god, Vishnu will see him through the troubles of this life and will also make possible final union of one's atman with Vishnu (who here is identified with the Paramatman) by means of his divine power. In the fourth chapter of the Gita, Vishnu, in the form of Krishna, delivers these words in answer to a question about his true nature, asked by the warrior hero, Arjuna. Krishna speaks:

> Manifold the renewals of my birth
> Have been, Arjuna! and of thy births, too!
> But mine I know, and thine thou knowest not,
> O Slayer of thy Foes! Albeit I be
> Unborn, undying, indestructible,
> The Lord of all things living; not the less—

By Maya, by my magic which I stamp
On floating Nature-forms, the primal vast—
I come, and go, and come. When Righteousness
Declines, O Bharata! when Wickedness
Is strong, I rise, from age to age, and take
Visible shape, and move a man with men,
Succoring the good, thrusting the evil back,
And setting Virtue on her seat again.
Who knows the truth touching my births on earth
And my divine work, when he quits the flesh
Puts on its load no more, falls no more down
To earthly birth: to Me he comes, dear Prince! [11]

By devotion to Vishnu as manifested in his avatar, Krishna, the tremendous gap between man in this maya world and the awesome, transcendent Paramatman is bridged. Without renouncing the world—in fact, by living in the midst of this changing scene—one can still achieve saving help and the peace which overcomes the vicissitudes of this life.

The devotees of Shiva also have divine help offered them, but in a different form. This deity is somewhat akin to the Baal god of the Old Testament in that his shakti represents the sexual potency which energizes life. This potency is made available in the form of the female energy of the consorts of Shiva. These are especially Kali, the "black one," and Durga, the "inaccessible one." Shiva, as Lord of Death, along with his wives, is able to answer the calls for help on the part of his followers. If a child is dying, if smallpox threatens, if demonic beings are at work, the god Shiva and his consorts will come to the saving help of those who turn to them in trust.

Even though both of these gods are but emanations, or maya forms, of the World-soul, for this very reason they are able to be concerned with man's plight. And by identifying oneself either with the god Vishnu or with Shiva one is really identifying himself with the Paramatman. The ecstasy of the wor-

[11] Lines 14-31. Edwin Arnold, tr., *The Song Celestial, or Bhagavad-Gītā.*

75

shiper of Krishna or of Kali is therefore considered akin to the flash of knowledge which frees those who follow the way of knowledge. "I am Vishnu," or "I am Kali," or "tat tvam asi" are all considered to be valid experiences of salvation.

*Salvation in Buddhism.* Since Buddhism is a Hindu heresy, there is much in the teachings of Gautama, the Buddha, that reflects his Hindu background. We have noted earlier that the Buddha denied the monism of the Upanishads with its view of the Paramatman as underlying all existence, and that he posited instead a dualism with a material world inhabited by purusha beings. The teaching of the Buddha about salvation starts with the assumption that man is a purusha reborn into this world because of past karma. After his experience of enlightenment the Buddha taught the famous Four Noble Truths about the nature of existence and the way to salvation. Although there is an early and simple formula stating this teaching, it might be well for us to look at these truths in a more analytical form.

The four truths are something like a syllogism in logic or even like a mathematical equation. Each truth leads simply into the next so that they all stand together. The first truth is the equation that "to live *is* to suffer." It is not simply that life involves or includes the element of suffering, but the completely radical affirmation that to live in this world means of necessity that one does suffer.

"This, monks, is the Noble Truth of Suffering: birth is suffering; decay is suffering; illness is suffering; death is suffering; presence of objects we hate is suffering; separation from objects we love is suffering; not to obtain what we desire is suffering." [12]

At this point a prior question might occur to the Western reader. If to live at all in this world means that one suffers, how did we get here in the first place? Although the Buddha does not answer this question, it appears that the answer to this "unanswerable" question is that ignorance in the past

[12] Brewster, *Life of Gotama*, in Hamilton, *Buddhism*, p. 29.

somehow has caused the life-stream (purusha) of an individual to originate and to start a cycle of births. But the Buddha, like other great religious teachers, was concerned first of all with man's present plight and a solution to this plight. Man is in fact in existence and therefore suffers. How to erase suffering and stop rebirth is the problem, not why we are here in the first place nor what happens after death.

The second of the Four Noble Truths is that of the cause of suffering. This is claimed to be rooted in craving or desire (tanha). This craving "causes the renewal of becomings, is accompanied by sensual delight, and seeks satisfaction now here, now there; that is to say, craving for pleasures, craving for becoming, craving for not becoming." [13] Thus any attachment to this world, any assertion of self, any desire to live and enjoy life causes suffering.

The third Noble Truth teaches the way to cessation of suffering. This is "passionlessness, cessation without remainder of this very craving; the laying aside of, the giving up, the being free from, the harboring no longer of, this craving." [14] If craving can be laid aside or left behind, suffering will cease and peace and contentment will characterize the saved man.

The fourth Noble Truth is the way to achieve this goal and is called the Noble Eightfold Path. This consists of eight ascending levels of thought and action called right views, right intent, right speech, right conduct, right means of livelihood, right endeavor, right mindfulness, and right meditation. Though each of these English phrases represents Sanskrit words which carry strong emotional connotations and subtle meanings which escape the Westerner, in essence they affirm that one can, in this life, break or cancel the bonds which hold one to existence. By practicing neither extreme asceticism (bodily discipline) nor self-indulgence, but by treading the middle way between these two, and by following single-mindedly the Noble Eightfold Path, one can become enlight-

[13] Ibid.
[14] Ibid.

ened in this life and have the hope of cessation of rebirths at death.

This experience of enlightenment is sometimes called *moksha*, or release, but more commonly is referred to by the difficult term *nirvāna*. This Sanskrit word has a different meaning in each Indian religion or sect, but its basic meaning always seems to indicate a loss of selfhood, of the ending of the delusion that one is a unique or separate entity. The root *vā* means *to blow*, and the prefix *nir* means negation. Thus the term can mean, to blow out, or to wane away. Then the self, with its passions and its delusions, wanes away and is replaced by light, truth, and selflessness. The man who is filled with fears, is tortured by cravings, and is living without hope can, by following the teachings of the Buddha, experience the salvation of nirvana while still in this present life. One early Buddhist monk gave expression to his experience of enlightenment or release in this way:

> I heard the Truth which that Great One had taught,
> And felt its mighty virtues, known by Him
> Who all things with supernal insight knew.
> The Path for winning things ambrosial
> I found. Past-master He in sooth to guide
> Into the way of blest security.[15]

The important element to notice in the Buddha's teaching about man's salvation is that it is essentially self-achieved. There are no gods who can help man in his plight. This is not to deny that gods exist, but such as there are in the heavenly realms are in the same plight as man. They are simply beings who have been reborn into the heavenly spheres instead of upon earth. In fact, it is taught that the Buddha himself had been reborn as a god more than once, but that rebirth in this present world as a human was a prerequisite to achieving

[15] Mrs. Rhys Davids, tr., *Psalms of the Early Buddhists: II.—Psalms of the Brethren* (2nd ed.; London: Oxford University Press, 1937), p. 70.

nirvana.[16] This lack of divine help was a limiting factor in the appeal of Buddhism, for although the Buddha's way of salvation was open to all, like the way of knowledge of the Upanishads it made certain demands involving serious study and meditation and also called upon the convert to renounce all normal ties with family and society. Gautama, the Buddha, had succeeded in his quest for enlightenment partly because of the merit he had accumulated in previous lives, but also because he was uniquely the Buddha.[17] But from earliest times Buddhism has been divided into a lay community of those who are not ready in this life to renounce the world, and the community of Arhats, or "worthy ones," the monks and nuns who have severed their ties with society. The layman accumulates merit by righteous living and supporting the monastic communities with gifts and alms.

In Southern Asia right down to our day when a person decides to renounce the world and to tread the Path of the Buddha he applies for admission to the Sangha (the Order, or monastery) and publicly renounces the world, taking vows of chastity and poverty. He then is asked to repeat the "Three Refuges": "I go for refuge to the Buddha. I go for refuge to the Dhamma. I go for refuge to the Sangha." This ancient affirmation represents the threefold help that is available to the one seeking Buddhist salvation. There is first the Buddha, who has shown by his life that it is possible to achieve nirvana, and thereby serves as an exemplar. The Dhamma (dharma) is the religious law, a compendium of rules to guide one in the monastic life. The Sangha itself sustains and guides the applicant in his search for salvation. Even though Buddhist salvation is "self-achieved," it is neither a lonely way nor without support and guidance. Buddhism has become one of the three

[16] From earliest times some women claimed to achieve enlightenment, and an early order of nuns was formed, but birth as a male was, and is, considered an asset in one's search for salvation.

[17] "Gotama the Buddha was the Buddha because he was Buddha, the Enlightened One, and he who cannot accept this premise will never know more than the shell of Buddhism." Christmas Humphreys, *Buddhism* (Baltimore: Penguin Books, 1951), p. 25.

79

great missionary religions of the world, and in chapter seven we will discuss its outreach and influence in East Asia.

*Salvation in Chinese religions.* It is a long leap from the world view of India to the tolerant humanism of China, but we turn now to consider the doctrine of man and of his salvation in Taoism and Confucianism. Confucius himself will be studied in chapter six, but the school of political and moral philosophy which bears his name represents a basic world view which offers an adjustment to the problems of existence which is a major part of the heritage of almost one fourth of the world's population.

Confucius (551-479 B.C.) lived in a feudal age in which warfare between rival, petty states was the order of the day. In fact, the whole period from Confucius' day to the end of the Chou Dynasty (211 B.C.) was plagued with constant warfare, famine and disease, and concomitant social instability. Both the Taoist and Confucian schools which arose in this period agreed that the reason the world "was going to the dogs" was that the way of Heaven and the way of the ancients had been ignored.

The Taoists, for their part, took the position that the way of the ancients was a sort of Garden of Eden, only more thickly populated than the one in Genesis. The Taoist philosopher, Chuang Tzu (died about 275 B.C.), told several parables to illustrate this teaching of the Taoist school. He pictured the golden age of the past as a time when all the world lived in peace and plenty. Men and animals went their own way unmolested. Men had no economic or political strife because there was neither civilization nor political states to attempt to discipline and control people against their true nature. The people were governed well because they were not governed at all. Into this idyllic situation, they claimed, the Confucianists inserted teachings about duty to one's neighbor and about filial piety, with the result that strife and confusion arose. Man's plight was caused by his attempts to make rules and laws to run society. The Taoists' solution was to revert to the way of the ancients and to live naturally, in a quietistic manner, unspoiled by civilization and government.[18]

This solution never commended itself to the Chinese in any thoroughgoing way. Instead the position of the Confucianists was followed. This school agreed with the Taoists that the problems confronting man were due to a turning from the way of the ancients. The difference was in how this ancient way was conceived and defined. The Taoists held that the natural way was the ideal to follow, while Confucianism claimed that the way of the ancestors was normative. They held that in ancient times the emperor obeyed the laws of heaven (t'ien) and all the people lived harmoniously together. The sons obeyed and respected their fathers, the wives loved and obeyed their husbands, the citizens were loyal to the emperor, and the emperor followed the natural law of heaven. All was peace and harmony, and the emperor was a philosopher king.

With this feudal ideal as the presupposition of the Confucianists, we are able to understand their teaching on the nature of man, his present need, and the solution to his needs—of his salvation. It is that mankind has turned from the way of the ancients out of ignorance and parental neglect. If people but knew the way of the ancients and followed it, all would be well. It is for this reason that Confucius said that he did not consider himself an innovator but rather a conserver of the past.

"The Master said, I have 'transmitted what was taught to me without making up anything of my own.' I have been faithful to and loved the Ancients." [19]

If man is part of the natural order of things (in the early Confucian system we find no sophisticated metaphysics about body, spirit, or consciousness), and if neglect has caused man's present plight, man is neither wicked nor evil; he is merely ignorant and misled. Education in the way of the ancients and the following of the proper order of things as there defined

[18] Cf. Giles, *Chuang Tzu*, chaps. IX and XI.
[19] Waley, *Analects*, VII:1.

will solve all problems. As the great Confucian interpreter, Mencius (372-289 B.C.), said:

In years of prosperity, most of the young people are well behaved, and in bad years, most of the young people turn to violence. This is not due to a difference in their natural endowments from Heaven, but because something has happened to lead their hearts astray. Take, for instance, the growing of wheat. You sow the seeds and till the field. The different plants are planted at the same time and grow from the same piece of land, and soon they sprout beautifully from the earth. When the time for harvest comes, they are all ripe, and although there is a difference between the different stalks of wheat, it is due to the difference in the soil, in the obtaining of moisture from the rain and the dew, and to differences in human care. Therefore, all who belong to the same species are essentially alike. Why should you doubt that this holds true also of human beings? The Sages belong to the same species as ourselves. . . . Therefore I say there is a common love for flavors in our mouths, a common sense for sounds in our ears, and a common sense for beauty in our eyes. Why then do we refuse to admit that there is something common in our souls also? What is that thing that we have in common in our souls? It is reason and a sense of right. The Sage is the man who has first discovered what is common to men's souls. Therefore, reason and the sense of right please our minds as beef and mutton and pork please our palates.[20]

On this basis the Confucian school sought to redeem society from errors and problems by a plan with two goals. The first goal was to create or train the *chün tzu*, or ideal man. This term means literally "sons of the princes," or the nobility. Confucius appears to have substituted an educated elite for the feudal gentry which based the noble class on birth. Only the scholar, he taught, could approach the ideal of the chün tzu, and, therefore, the ideal ruler was the sage king. The other goal of this philosophy was to create an ideal society modeled on the way of the ancients in which Heaven, the ruler, and society—all were acting in harmony.

[20] Lin Yutang, *The Wisdom of Confucius* (New York: The Modern Library, 1938), pp. 281-82.

The only problem to one who is not a follower of Confucius appears to be the two Confucian assumptions—that there was a way of the ancients which actually conformed to what was claimed for it and which could be known, and the assumption that all men naturally want to do the good and only need to be told about it. But for 2,500 years Confucianism has been a creative and stabilizing force in Chinese history.

## Man's Plight and Salvation in Some Major Faiths

We began this discussion of salvation with the assumption that man, as a religious animal, finds himself confronted with forces and events which all too often frustrate him in his struggle to find meaning and security in life. We have described how the different religions ascribe the sources of this frustration to various causes and offer varying solutions to man's plight. The wide variety of causes and solutions raises once again the question as to whether all religions are fundamentally the same or whether they are really quite different.

For primitive man the world is terrifyingly alive with mana power, an amoral force which he must channel and control if he is to survive. Such means as tabus, fetishes, and various forms of magic are employed to coerce mana to work for the good of the tribe and to ward off its evil effects. The welfare of the individual is subordinated to that of the tribe.

For the Jew, Christian, and Muslim man's plight is due primarily to his abuse of his God-given freedom by willful disobedience. To achieve salvation man must serve his creator and seek the gracious help of God in order to be able to face the overwhelming issues of life with any hope of victory. God has revealed his will for man through Moses, Jesus, or Muhammad, and salvation is to be found in obeying that revealed will.

In India the Hindu begins with the assumption of rebirth as caused by one's deeds in a previous life, and with man's plight as resulting primarily from the isolation of his atman from the Paramatman which leads him to suffer a cycle of

births in maya existence. Salvation is to be achieved in one of
several ways: through overcoming ignorance of man's true
nature by the way of knowledge found in the Upanishads; by
the way of works, that is, through the strict following of one's
dharma, or duty, predetermined by birth; or by turning to
Vishnu or Shiva for gracious help to overcome the terrors and
vicissitudes of life.

The Buddha accepted the Hindu teachings of karma and
rebirth, but defined man's plight, not as the isolation of the
atman from a World-soul, but rather as the fact of existence
itself in a real world, in which to live is to suffer. Salvation
is self-achieved and is to be found in understanding one's existence in terms of the Four Noble Truths and in following
the Noble Eightfold Path of the Buddha.

In China both Taoism and Confucianism agree in ascribing
man's plight to a turning from the ancient ways, but for the
Taoist it was a turning from the Way of the natural order of
the universe, while for Confucius it was a turning from the
way of the ancient, idealized feudal order. The remedy, or
way to salvation, offered by each religion was to recover the
true way of life. For the Taoist this meant that one should
learn the Tao Tê, or virtuous Way of the universe; for Confucius it meant a stress on recovering the ancient, feudal way
in which true nobility was to be found in character as ex-
emplified by the "sage king."

If we use the phrase "circles of faith" to describe the above
differing positions, one further problem presents itself. This
is the observation that each circle of faith has its own "built-
in" inconsistencies which are to be traced back to the axiomatic assumptions with which each religion begins. This may
be illustrated by a brief discussion of the vexing "problem of
evil" with which theologians in the biblical faiths continually
wrestle.

That no one can solve the problem of evil is a truism that
bears repeating. One can shout that pain and fear do not exist,
but not many will listen. One can say that what appears to be
evil is really good in the greater plan of God, but that is a

statement of faith rather than obvious fact. But it might be instructive to inquire what some of these religions do with this problem, to ask what "solution" is offered to the problem of evil and the fact of man's inhumanity to man.

It is interesting that the Hindu and the Buddhist consider the Christian doctrine of forgiveness a monstrous doctrine. They claim that it is unjust to teach that one can commit grievous sins and then be forgiven without penalty. Why is this basic Christian theme so regarded? It is because rebirth in this present life is itself regarded as the just punishment for all that one has done, good and evil, in previous lives. To the question put to Jesus, "Why was this man born blind?" [21] the Hindu would say, because of past karma. A deed once done cannot be forgiven, but must instead be worked off in existence. A modern Buddhist says, "For sin to be 'forgiven' is as impossible as for virtue to forego its reward, for the Path is lit by the ever-deepening foreglow of its goal. To depart from the Path is its own punishment, for the steps must, at *whatever cost*, be retraced." [22]

But this quarrel between one in the Indian tradition and one in the Palestinian fold is fruitless, simply because each side is merely illustrating its own presuppositions, tacit or even unexamined. The Confucianist might enter the fray with the simple affirmation that evil is in the world because the "way of the ancients" had been forgotten or ignored. But what concern would a Hindu or a Jew have for the way of the Chinese emperors Wen and Wu? And what does the Buddhist know of Yahweh who led the children of Israel out of bondage and called them to obey the covenant?

Perhaps enough has been said to clarify and to document still further our thesis. Man's search for salvation, for meaning in life, is always within the context of the circle of his faith. The presuppositions or axioms about the nature of man, of this present world, and the way to find security and hope

[21] John 9:1 ff.
[22] Edmond Holmes, *The Creed of the Buddha*, p. 94, quoted in Humphreys, *Buddhism*, p. 109.

in a hostile world are all of a piece in each case. They are found within the circle of faith which characterizes each religion. Whether a man can save himself, nay, must save himself, is obviously radically different from the position that man cannot save himself but must rely upon the grace and power of a god.

# CHAPTER 4

# WHY DO
# THE GOOD?

Those who have only the vaguest acquaintance with the scriptures of the nonbiblical religions have heard the statement that "each great religion has a Ten Commandments." Anthologies of scriptures often stress the ethical element in the faiths of mankind, perhaps quoting a "Golden Rule" from most of the religions. Usually this is done to support the contention that, at least in the area of the good life, the great religions are at heart the same. This position can be expressed in statements such as the following:

"Since the different religions agree in the area of ethical teachings, why don't people forget their differences in matters of faith and belief and learn to cooperate in the area of ethical living?"

"After all, who am I to say that my religion is better than another's—isn't the Buddhist or the Muslim just as good as I am?"

The claim that ethics is the common denominator of the world's religions has a good deal of force behind it simply because it is "on the side of the angels." For is it not laudatory that there are, for instance, so many Christians who today desire to minimize the differences between their religion and other religions in the interest of developing one world?

A well-known anthologist of the scriptures of the world's religions, Lewis Browne, stated the position of the "liberal" on this subject quite baldly in the introduction to his selection of sacred writings. He said that in his choice of passages:

> The entire emphasis is on the ethical element in each religion, on the moral laws and preachments.
> Here is the reason. What we need is a keener awareness of the kinship between religions, and nowhere is this kinship so marked as on the ethical level. Men may differ grossly in what and how they worship, but not in why and how they believe they should behave. They may be divided by that which their priests assert to be divine, but not by what their prophets prescribe as humane.[1]

Apart from other considerations this position leaves out one entire dimension of the science of ethics, of the theory of the good life. This dimension is that of motivation, the sanctions for an ethic. That is, it ignores the question as to why one should live a good life. It is a position that apparently was offered with the best of intentions, since it appears to have been predicated upon the Jewish background of Mr. Browne, which included the biblical affirmation that religion and morality are synonymous. But this is not true for all religions, as, for instance, it was not true for the followers of the Baal cult of the Old Testament Canaanites.

But even if there should be agreement upon the content of ethical living, it does not necessarily follow that two religions which agree in this one area really are the same. It is possible for them to be very different in areas that matter greatly, such as whether or not there is a god to be obeyed. Communism, for instance, denies the personal God of the Bible, yet at the same time it reflects the Judaic background of Karl Marx in its concern for the improvement of life for all men in this present age, and it also points toward a utopian goal akin to the

[1] The World's Great Scriptures (New York: The Macmillan Company, 1946), p. xv.

Christian dream of the kingdom of God on earth. Perhaps both the obvious truth of Browne's position and also my reservations about it can be made explicit if I quote from a mimeographed letter sent me many years ago. It was dated August 25, 1938; it came from the office of the Young Communist League of Los Angeles, and was signed by the County League President. It read as follows:

Dear Friend:

Large sections of Christian young people interested in realizing the social gospel of Christ, have adopted the watchword and set as their goal, "Christian Youth Building a New World." The goal of building a new and better world is one to which all right thinking young people must generously respond. Young Communists share this goal in common with Christian young people and other wide sections of American youth. We are convinced that greater mutual understanding between young Christians and young Communists will make possible rapid strides towards the attainment of that better social order.

On Sunday evening, August 28th at the Olympic Auditorium Earl Browder, General Secretary of the Communist Party and William Z. Foster, its Chairman, will speak to the people of Los Angeles. We feel that you, as a Christian young person, will be interested in hearing [what] they have to say concerning the Communist attitude toward the immediate and pressing social problems which we are mutually interested in solving. We feel certain that in the persons of these outstanding Communist leaders you will find much to respect, and in the ideas they present, much to stimulate your thinking and much with which to agree.

Don't take other peoples' words for what Communists, old and young, stand for! Find out for yourself!

This appeal was made at the time when the Communist line was pleading for a united front against fascism—and also not too long before the infamous Hitler-Stalin pact. It also was toward the end of the period during which many Christian leaders had been stressing the close agreement between the ethical and social demands of prophetic Christianity and the

89

teachings of Marxism.[2] It was a sore temptation to many of us to accept the Communist line, and to tone down or even abandon differences in the area of beliefs, in our earnestness to further good works among men. For this appeal was directed not only to Christian youth but also to all young Americans who had been thoroughly indoctrinated into accepting as axiomatic the value of the pragmatic approach to life. Thus any emphasis upon the practical side of religion, upon the ethical fruits of faith, was held to be the real test of the validity of that faith.

Fortunately for many of us, our Christian professors and leaders in the various Christian youth movements had made us aware of the gulf which separates the Christian church from communism. The necessity of understanding one's faith had not been ignored, and the problem of differing beliefs had not been neglected. We were taught that the means that are used must be consistent with the desired ends, and that there is a difference between regarding man as an economic animal and believing that he is a child of God. Some of my acquaintances, on the other hand, accepted this sort of appeal from the Young Communist League and became fellow travelers, or even members of the Communist party. Perhaps this is one reason why I feel so strongly about this problem of the apparent similarity between ethical teachings in the world's religions.

## Ethics and Religion

Any ethical system has two main parts. In the first place there is the substance of what a particular tradition considers to be right and wrong in thought and action. Such injunctions as "do not steal," "do not indulge in intoxicants," "do not covet," or "love your enemies" give expression to the content of normative behavior. It is this portion of ethical instruction that appears to be so similar in different religious traditions.

[2] Cf., e.g., John Macmurray, *Creative Society* (New York: Association Press, 1936).

But the other part of an ethical system has to do with the reason *why* one should do the good. Here the question is not *what* should I do, but *why* I should do that which is demanded. "*Why* should I not steal, or *why* should I love my enemies?" And even more to the point is the question, "What happens if I just live my own selfish life and take what I can for myself?" This second aspect of ethics, of the reason *why* one should live a good life, is known technically as a concern for sanctions.

At the risk of sounding pedantic the definition of an ethical sanction as given in the *Oxford English Dictionary* is here quoted: an ethical sanction is defined as "a consideration which operates to enforce obedience to any law or rule of conduct; a recognized motive for conformity to moral or religious law, operating either through the agent's desire for some resultant good or through his fear of some resultant evil."

Now it is precisely here that the real issue lies. The young Communist making an appeal for Christian cooperation in a program of social reform does well to leave out any mention of means, motive, or belief. For this is what separates the Christian from the Communist. If we limit our consideration of ethics to the content of the ethic, it is true that we are struck by strong similarities. But since ethical systems also involve the question of sanctions, and since each system has its own context of faith, or view of man and the world, any fair approach to this question must include this significant other half of the problem. Let us see how the claim that all great religions have much the same ethic holds up under analysis.

### The Maxim Known as the "Golden Rule"

A great deal has been written about the Golden Rule as found in the words of Jesus since there is such widespread occurrence of similar forms of this maxim. It usually is quoted as it appears in the Sermon on the Mount: "Whatever you wish that men would do to you, do so to them; for this is the law and the prophets." [3] The most famous parallel to Jesus' word is the saying ascribed to Confucius. In the *Analects* we read: "Tzu-kung asked saying, Is there any single saying that one can act upon all day and every day? The Master said, Perhaps the saying about consideration: 'Never do to others what you would not like them to do to you.' " [4] These two teachings appear to say basically the same thing about how one should act in his dealings with other persons. What, then, of the context of the ethic in each case, and what of the sanctions, stated or implied, for both biblical and Chinese thought?

*The Golden Rule in biblical thought.* The saying of Jesus, reported both in the Gospel of Matthew and of Luke, appears to be an independent or "floating" teaching of a proverbial nature since in each case it concludes a short collection of related sayings. [5] It is reported that Rabbi Hillel, whose ministry was about a generation before that of Jesus, was asked by a heathen to be taught "the whole Torah while he stood on one foot." His answer was: "What is hateful to you, do not to your neighbor: that is the whole Torah, while the rest is the commentary thereof; go and learn it." [6] Actually it has been demonstrated that this saying was not original with Hillel but was already proverbial. [7] Some Christians have argued that Hillel's statement is inferior to that of Jesus since Hillel used the negative form of command. But, as George Foot Moore has pointed out, this argument is both misleading and beside the point. [8]

Instead we are concerned to ask what meaning this teaching has in the context of Judaism as well as in the teaching of Jesus. Biblical religion always has as its central principle God's will for man. Both for Rabbi Hillel and for Jesus the essential

[3] Matt. 7:12.

[4] Waley, XV:23.

[5] In Matthew it is found in the Sermon on the Mount; in Luke in the Sermon on the Plain.

[6] The Babylonian Talmud, *Shabbat* 31a (Soncino ed., p. 140).

[7] Cf. George Foot Moore, *Judaism* (Cambridge: Harvard University Press, 1927), II, 87-88.

[8] *Ibid.*, p. 88.

meaning of the Golden Rule is rooted in their faith in the creator God who has made all men. One's fellow man, therefore, should be regarded as a fellow child of God. In the eighth century B.C., the Judean prophet Micah proclaimed:

> He has showed you, O man, what is good;
> and what does the LORD require of you
> but to do justice, and to love kindness,
> and to walk humbly with your God?[9]

In this same prophetic strain Jesus also based love for one's neighbor upon complete devotion to God.

And one of the scribes came up and heard them disputing with one another, and seeing that he answered them well, asked him, "Which commandment is the first of all?" Jesus answered, "The first is, 'Hear, O Israel: The Lord our God, the Lord is one; and you shall love the Lord your God with all your heart, and with all your soul, and with all your mind, and with all your strength.' The second is this, 'You shall love your neighbor as yourself.' There is no other commandment greater than these.[10]

The question of *why* I should treat others as I would like to be treated, and what this means in terms of my attitude toward my fellow man, is stated uncompromisingly to be based on my service to God. And this service to God requires that I love even those who persecute me. But the sanction invoked is not merely the desire to serve and please God but includes also the knowledge that the God of Jesus is the final arbiter of man's destiny. Jesus said, "Do not fear those who kill the body but cannot kill the soul [that is, do not fear man]; rather fear him [God] who can destroy both soul and body in hell." [11] Or again, "If your right eye causes you to sin, pluck it out and throw it away; it is better that you lose one of your members than that your whole body be thrown into hell." [12]

[9] Mic. 6:8.
[10] Mark 12:28-31.
[11] Matt. 10:28.
[12] Matt. 5:29.

*The Golden Rule in Confucian thought.* When we turn to a consideration of Confucius' use of the Golden Rule we find that it also is stated negatively. Homer Dubs reminds us, however, that Confucius' "statement of the Golden Rule is negative only in form—Chinese style prefers a negative to a positive statement, saying that a thing is 'not-good' instead of 'bad,' etc." [13] Actually, as Professor Dubs goes on to point out, Confucius did give a positive interpretation to this teaching, but this is not our prime concern. Instead the pertinent question is: What is the context of Confucius' teaching of *shu*, a term which Mr. Waley has translated as "consideration," but which is usually translated as "reciprocity," which is expressed in the phrase "Never do to others what you would not like them to do to you." We find that Confucius' whole system was predicated upon an idealized feudal order in which every relationship of life was expected to follow a predetermined pattern. This ideal order was supposed to have existed in the legendary golden age of the Shang dynasty (c. 1500 B.C.). Then, it was believed, the nobles were just and kind and the common people peaceful and obedient. Everyone followed his proper station in life and harmony reigned in the family, in the community, and in the nation.

It is in this context of the ideal of the ancient feudal order that the term "others," in the Confucian form of the Golden Rule, is to be understood. We find that it actually had two meanings, depending upon the station of the person involved. The ideal society had five sets of relationships which, with their natural subdivisions, included every possible relationship between any two persons. And in each possible relationship there always is one who is *superior* and one who is *inferior*. The role of the inferior is to be characterized first of all by the attitude of filial piety (*hsiao*). The son is to be obedient and subservient to his father. The father in turn is to reciprocate (shu) with kindness and condescension. And so on for each

[13] "The Development of Altruism in Confucianism," *Philosophy East and West*, I, No. 1 (1951), 49.

relationship in life. The father as citizen is to be filial to the emperor, who is expected to respond with shu.

In the *Chung Yung*, or Central Harmony, a second-century B.C. Confucian writing, the following discourse is ascribed to Confucius:

Confucius remarked: "The moral law is not something away from the actuality of human life. . . .

"When a man carries out the principles of conscientiousness and reciprocity he is not far from the moral law. What you do not wish others should do unto you, do not do unto them.

"There are four things in the moral life of a man, not one of which I have been able to carry out in my life. To serve my father as I would expect my son to serve me: that I have not been able to do. To serve my sovereign as I would expect a minister under me to serve me: that I have not been able to do. To act towards my elder brother as I would expect my younger brother to act towards me: that I have not been able to do. To be the first to behave towards friends as I would expect them to behave towards me: that I have not been able to do." [14]

The conclusion would appear to be inescapable: The Confucian Golden Rule is not a statement of the proper relationship between equals but between two unequal parties, one superior, the other inferior. The following diagram might help illustrate this interpretation of the way in which the five relationships of life are basic to Confucian thought.

| A (Emperor) |
| --- |
| B (Father) |
| C (Son) |

In this diagram B expects filial piety from C and gives it to A. B reciprocates to C with kindness and justice and expects the same from A. But for the son to try to be paternalistic—

[14] *The Conduct of Life, or the Universal Order of Confucius: a translation of one of the Four Confucian Books, Hitherto Known as the Doctrine of the Mean,* tr. by Ku Hung Ming, The Wisdom of the East Series (London: John Murray, 1908), pp. 25-26.

to have an attitude of *jen* ("benevolent love") for his father, or for the father to have such for the emperor was out of the question.[15] On the other hand, the emperor could not have an attitude of filial piety for his subjects, nor could the father have such an attitude for his son. This would be a confusion of roles. In fact, because such confusion in society did exist, Confucius called for a "rectification of names" so that each person would begin to have the attitudes proper to his station in life. And in this ideal society one's responsibility and his response to others would vary with his relationship to the other person.

### The Ten Commandments in the Bible and in Buddhism

It is to be hoped that enough has been said to support the contention that the mere quoting of similar teachings in different religions out of context is both misleading and mistaken. Let us continue the documentation of our thesis by examining another form of ethical instruction which has attracted much attention and has also resulted in much confused commentary. This is the occurrence in several religions of a "Ten Commandments." Again we will compare the biblical form of this ethical teaching with that of one other religion, in this case, Buddhism.

*The biblical Ten Commandments* appear in two different sources in the Pentateuch, the "D" source of about 650 B.C. (Deut. 5:6-21), and the "P" (Priestly) source, dated about 450 B.C. (Exod. 20:2-17). Although the two Decalogues agree in the basic prohibitions, they reflect quite different points of view in the reasons given for their observance—in the sanctions employed for the teachings. The most significant difference is found in the sanction for hallowing the seventh day. Thus the D source, with a prophetic concern for social justice, links remembrance of the Sabbath with the memory of Egyptian servitude. The Israelites are to give a day of rest to their servants and to remember that they too had once been

[15] Cf. Waley, *Analects*, pp. 27-29.

slaves in Egypt. The P source, with a cultic concern for Sabbath observance, bases this practice in the very creation of the world, wherein God made the world in six days and rested on the seventh day.

Without the commentary the Decalogue would read:

1. You shall have no other gods before me.
2. You shall not make yourself a graven image.
3. You shall not take the name of the LORD [Yahweh] your God in vain.
4. Remember the sabbath day, to keep it holy.
5. Honor your father and your mother.
6. You shall not kill.
7. You shall not commit adultery.
8. You shall not steal.
9. You shall not bear false witness against your neighbor.
10. You shall not covet.[16]

There is a lot of vague talk that one hears constantly that runs something like this. "If all the world obeyed the Ten Commandments we would have no more wars. If God's laws given to Moses on Mt. Sinai were taken seriously the United Nations Organization would have its problems solved." Actually such talk is neither biblical nor Christian. In the Sermon on the Mount we find, in the famous antitheses of Jesus, that the Ten Commandments are subordinated to a higher law. The prohibitions against such outward actions as murder and adultery are taken for granted as part of the way of life of any decent citizen. But Jesus expresses the demands of God in much stronger language—in the language of absolute obedience.

You have heard that it was said to the men of old, "You shall not kill; and whoever kills shall be liable to judgment." But I say to you that every one who is angry with his brother shall be liable to judgment; whoever insults his brother shall be liable to the council, and whoever says, "You fool!" shall be liable to the hell of fire. . . .

[16] Exod. 20:3-17, in part.

You have heard that it was said, "You shall not commit adultery." But I say to you that every one who looks at a woman lustfully has already committed adultery with her in his heart.[17]

But Judaism itself had long since taught that the Ten Commandments are but minimal to any religious life. We have already quoted the classic statement from Micah which is in the same prophetic tradition as Jesus' words in the Sermon on the Mount. Judaism had also developed the teaching of "the Law of the heart" which stressed obedience of the total man to God, rather than simply the outward actions of the Decalogue.[18] And Paul, the apostle to the Gentiles, is simply restating this high Jewish ethic in Christian terms when he claims that Christian love supersedes the Ten Commandments.

Owe no one anything, except to love one another; for he who loves his neighbor has fulfilled the law. The commandments, "You shall not commit adultery, You shall not kill, You shall not steal, You shall not covet," and any other commandment, are summed up in this sentence, "You shall love your neighbor as yourself." Love does no wrong to a neighbor; therefore love is the fulfilling of the law.[19]

Even though the Ten Commandments do not represent the highest form of Jewish or Christian ethics, it is necessary to examine both the context and the sanctions for these teachings in order to compare and contrast them with the Ten Commandments of Buddhism. For biblical man the context of the Ten Commandments is that they represent, at least in part, the will of Yahweh, creator of the world and of man. It has always proved necessary for any society to spell out the details of obedience, even though the majority of men know in general terms what it means to live ethically. And if one is to follow the will of God, it becomes necessary to state what

[17] Matt. 5:21-22, 27-28.
[18] Cf., e.g., Moore, *Judaism*, I, 251-62.
[19] Rom. 13:8-10; cf. Mark 10:17-22.

that will is. Starting with the assumption that one's salvation and highest good lie in obeying the will of God, the Ten Commandments represent a succinct statement of that will for man, at least in minimal form. In fact, both Judaism and Christianity have produced a vast body of ethical literature which in some ways could be regarded as a continuing commentary upon the Ten Commandments.

But the particular sanctions invoked by the Decalogue are also instructive for our purposes. Granting that the Jew and the Christian find expressed here the will of God for their lives, what are the positive and negative results for those who obey or disobey? Once again the answer is to be found in the wide context of belief in a creator God who also has power to save and to destroy, to reward and to punish.[20] In the Old Testament the Jewish Decalogue offers as a sanction for the fifth commandment: "Honor your father and your mother, as the Lord your God commanded you; *that your days may be prolonged, and that it may go well with you, in the land which the Lord your God gives you.*" [21] The italicized words serve to stress the teaching that if you obey these commandments as God's will for your life you will be rewarded by long life, peace, and prosperity. On the other hand, part of the sanction of the second commandment threatens punishment as the reason why "You shall not make for yourself a graven image, . . . for I the Lord your God am a jealous God, visiting the iniquity of the fathers upon the children to the third and the fourth generation of those who hate me." [22] In the Sermon on the Mount we find these sanctions expressed in terms of eternal rewards and punishments. Thus Jesus states that those who are persecuted on his account should "Rejoice and be glad, for your reward is great in heaven." [23] On the other hand, those who do not obey shall be cast into hell.[24]

*The Buddhist Ten Commandments.* Although there are

[20] Cf. above, pp. 19-20, and 34 ff.
[21] Deut. 5:16; cf. Exod. 20:12.
[22] Exod. 20:4-5, in part; cf. Deut. 5:8-10.
[23] Matt. 5:12.
[24] Cf., e.g., Matt. 25:41.

frequent references to the "fact" that all great religions have a Ten Commandments, the closest approximation in a non-biblical religion is the decalogue of Buddhism, with a close parallel to be found in the scriptures of its sister religion, Jainism. The Buddhist Ten Precepts are considered to be binding upon the monk who has renounced the world; the lay member who remains a member of society is bound only by the first five (except on fast days, when he is bound by all but the last).

The Buddhist monk must take the following vows:

1. Abstinence from destroying life.
2. Abstinence from taking what is not given.
3. Abstinence form unchastity.
4. Abstinence from falsehood.
5. Abstinence from spirituous liquors, strong drink, intoxicants, which are a cause of negligence.
6. Abstinence from eating at the wrong time [*i.e.,* after noon].
7. Abstinence from looking at dancing, singing, music, and plays.
8. Abstinence from wearing garlands, scents, unguents, ornaments, and adornments, which are a cause of negligence.
9. Abstinence from a high or large bed.
10. Abstinence from accepting gold and silver.[25]

It should be noted that apart from the prohibitions against killing (anything), stealing, unchastity (actually, for the monk *all* sexual activity is forbidden), and lying, there is no real parallel between these ten commandments and those of the Old Testament. What can be said is that there are ten rules; what is found in common is necessary as basic law in any society.

What is the context, the circle of faith, within which the Buddhist understands these Ten Precepts? From the Hinduism of his day the Buddha inherited the teachings of karma (deeds) and *samsara* (rebirth). But his analysis of man's

[25] *Buddhist Scriptures,* tr. by E. J. Thomas, The Wisdom of the East Series (London: John Murray, 1913), pp. 52-53.

religious situation was radically different from the main line of Hinduism.[26] He taught that man is reborn into this present life, partly because of ignorance which causes him to attach false values to life, but especially because of his cravings or thirsts (tanha). The Buddha's revolutionary teachings were reduced, in early tradition, to four propositions, the famous Four Noble Truths. The first truth is that "to live is to suffer." This means that existence is made up of birth, growth, decay, and death, to be followed by rebirth. To continue in this samsara is painful, and is without true meaning or value. The second truth is that suffering (and existence) is caused by desire or craving (tanha). This includes all the natural desires and feelings of life—hunger, sex, love, desire for pleasant things, security, good health, etc. This craving causes one to remain bound to existence and to rebirth. The third truth is that one can break the fetters which bind him to samsara by eliminating all craving, all desires. The fourth truth is that the way to freedom from craving and rebirth, from existence, is to follow the Noble Eightfold Path of right thought and action which will lead to the elimination of all desires. This in turn enables a Buddhist to eliminate ignorance and to achieve extinction of self with its thirsts and cravings and so to attain nirvana ("extinction" of self).

In practice the following of the Noble Eightfold Path means that one must seek to sever all attachments which bind one to this present world. There is no place for love for parents, attachment to friends or possessions, desire for fame or security, or for ascribing worth to anything in this world in which to live is to suffer. Only by radical renunciation of all such attachments can all desire and craving be erased. Buddhist ethics are concerned with this one thing: How can I think and act so as to avoid having any craving, desire, or attachment for any person or thing? How can I achieve this ideal of non-attachment so that I can avoid any bond which could keep

[26] Cf. above, pp. 22-23, and 76 ff.

me fastened to samsara, to the wheel of rebirth? Thus the Buddhist Ten Precepts do not represent the content of obedience to the will of god; they form instead a Buddhist summary of what is required to achieve self-salvation by following in the path of the Buddha. This is why the Buddhist Ten Commandments enjoin the Buddhist monk not to "use high or luxurious beds," nor to "accept gold or silver," nor to "indulge in intoxicants" nor "to destroy life." Those do not represent a way of obedience to a god who promises that "one's days will be long in the land." Instead they help make plain, and shed light on, the Noble Eightfold Path which leads to cessation of desire and finally to nirvana, to the waning away of the self. To maintain that the Ten Commandments of the Bible and of Buddhism represent the same ethic is either to presume upon the ignorance of the reader or to fly in the face of fact.

### Nonviolence in Biblical and Indian Religions

A final illustration of the problem of the relevance of faith to works, of the vital relationship which exists between motivation and conduct, concerns nonviolence when advocated as the proper method of resolving conflicts in personal and social relations. The pacifist movement in America, for instance, prior to World War II had strong support from large segments of the Christian church, not only from the historic peace churches but also from leaders of liberal Protestantism. The position was widely held that the true Christian way included perforce acceptance of pacifism and the rejection of all participation in armed conflict. The Civilian Public Service camps of World War II were in part a reflection of the strength of the Christian pacifist movement.

But the most famous practitioner of nonviolent coercion in the first half of this century was Mohandas K. Gandhi, a leader in the struggle to drive the British rule from India. Through following his career the West became familiar with such terms as *ahimsa* (not-harming) and *satya-graha* (soul-force). In America the sit-down strikes of the C.I.O. in the 1930's and the nonviolent sit-in demonstrations of the Negro in the 1960's led by the Reverend Martin Luther King, Jr., illustrate Gandhi's influence. In the following discussion we are concerned, not with the complex question of peace and war, but only with the factor of motivation for those who advocate the way of nonviolence, either in the biblical or the Indian religious tradition.

*Nonviolence in biblical thought.* We have noted above that biblical faith presupposes a creator God and teaches that man is a creature whose duty it is to obey his creator. The Hebrew God is also Lord of history, and man's hope of salvation therefore lies under God's sovereignty. The biblical teaching that one should forgive his enemies and love them is based on these presuppositions. The prophet Jeremiah, a few years after the first group of Jews had been carried to exile in Babylon by King Nebuchadnezzar in 598 B.C., wrote the exiles a letter urging them, in the name of God, to "seek the welfare of the city where I [God] have sent you into exile, and pray to the LORD on its behalf, for in its welfare you will find your welfare." [27] But his urging that the Jews collaborate with their mortal enemies is followed by the promise: "For thus says the LORD: When seventy years are completed for Babylon, I will visit you, and I will fulfil to you my promise and bring you back to this place. For I know the plans I have for you, says the LORD, plans for welfare and not for evil, to give you a future and a hope. Then you will call upon me and come and pray to me, and I will hear you." [28]

So too, the beautiful teaching of Isaiah of Babylon during the Exile,[29] that Israel has been chosen to be the LORD's suffering servant who is to lead all nations to God by means of her obedience in suffering, is linked with the view that this

[27] Jer. 29:7.
[28] Jer. 29:10-12.
[29] Called "Deutero-Isaiah," Isaiah, chapters 40–55, c. 550 B.C.

God alone is worthy of service and that he alone can save his chosen people.

> "You are my witnesses," says the LORD,
>   "and my servant whom I have chosen,
> that you may know and believe me
>   and understand that I am He.
> Before me no god was formed,
>   nor shall there be any after me.
> I, I am the LORD,
>   and besides me there is no savior. . . ."
> Thus says the LORD,
>   your Redeemer, the Holy One of Israel:
> "For your sake I will send to Babylon
>   and break down all the bars,
>   and the shouting of the Chaldeans
>     will be turned to lamentations." [30]

In the New Testament Jesus' familiar words are in this same context of obedience to God as Lord of life:

You have heard that it was said, "You shall love your neighbor and hate your enemy." But I say to you, Love your enemies and pray for those who persecute you, so that you may be sons of your Father who is in heaven; for he makes his sun rise on the evil and on the good, and sends rain on the just and on the unjust. . . . You, therefore, must be perfect, as your heavenly Father is perfect.[31]

In every case these biblical passages appear to say that if man does his duty to God and trusts God, the way of forgiveness and selfless love will be rewarded by God who alone has final power over the affairs of men.

*In Buddhism* the motivation for nonviolence and the practice of love as the law of life also require that one live a selfless existence, but here the goal is nirvana, extinction of self, rather than fulfillment of the true self by service to a god. In the Dhammapada we read:

[30] Isa. 43:10-11, 14.
[31] Matt. 5:43-45, 48.

"He abused me, he beat me, he defeated me, he robbed me," the hatred of those who do not harbour such thoughts is not appeased.

"He abused me, he beat me, he defeated me, he robbed me," the hatred of those who do not harbour such thoughts is appeased.

Hatreds never cease by hatred in this world; by love alone they cease. This is an ancient law.

The others know not that in this quarrel we perish; those of them who realize it have their quarrels calmed thereby.[32]

Buddhist teachings of nonviolence, and even of positive love, do not permit one to love others in a personal and sympathetic manner. Instead the Buddha taught that man must form no attachments with the world.

Consort not with those that are dear, nor ever with those that are not dear; not seeing those that are dear and the sight of those that are not dear, are both painful.

Hence hold nothing dear, for separation from those that are dear is bad: bonds do not exist for those to whom nought is dear or not dear.

From endearment springs grief, from endearment springs fear; for him who is wholly free from endearment there is no grief, much less fear.[33]

*Noninjury in Hinduism.* When we turn to Hinduism from early Buddhism we find that the mainstream of Hinduism is monistic.[34] There is a single principle, the Paramatman, or World-soul, which represents all that truly is. Man is considered to be composed of an atman (breath or soul) which is a portion of the Paramatman, which is combined with a body composed of *gunas* (material "strands" or essences). Each atman is reborn into this present maya existence (from mā, to measure or limit) which is limited both in space and time. Whereas man's atman is eternal, his present physical

---

[32] Nārada Thera, tr. The Wisdom of the East Series (London: John Murray, 1954), pp. 15-16 (*Yamakavagga*, vss. 3-6).

[33] *Ibid.*, p. 58 (*Piyavagga*, vss. 210-12).

[34] Cf. above, pp. 21-22, and 69 ff.

existence, attached to a maya body, is illusory, without final reality.

The most famous passage in Hindu scriptures dealing with the problem of killing and of the violence of war is found in the opening chapters of the *Bhagavad-Gita,* "The Song of the Lord," which is contained in the epic of the Bharata war, the *Mahabharata* (c. first century A.D.). The setting of the *Gita* (the Song) pictures one of the five Bharata brothers, Arjuna, who is also a peerless warrior, discussing the coming battle with his charioteer, Krishna. The battle is to be with Arjuna's cousins, the Kurus, to determine who shall rule the kingdom of India, and Arjuna knows that if he participates in the battle he must kill many of his kinsmen. Arjuna asks Krishna whether it is right to fight, and therefore slay, and what possible value such senseless slaughter can have. In the course of the Gita Krishna reveals himself to Arjuna as none other than a manifestation (avatar) of the great god Vishnu, who has taken the form of a charioteer. But in the dialogue the underlying Hindu interpretation of the meaning of war and violence is made clear. Arjuna speaks:

> "Krishna! as I behold, come here to shed
> Their common blood, yon concourse of our kin,
> My members fail, my tongue dries in my mouth,
> A shudder thrills my body, and my hair
> Bristles with horror; from my weak hand slips
> Gandiv, the goodly bow; a fever burns
> My skin to parching; hardly may I stand;
> The life within me seems to swim and faint;
> Nothing do I foresee save woe and wail!
> It is not good, O Keshev! nought of good
> Can spring from mutual slaughter! . . ." [35]

Krishna replies:

> "Thou grievest where no grief should be! thou speak'st
> Words lacking wisdom! for the wise in heart

Mourn not for those that live, nor those that die.
Nor I, nor thou, nor any one of these,
Ever was not, nor ever will not be,
For ever and for ever afterwards. . . .
    The soul which is not moved,
The soul that with a strong and constant calm
Takes sorrow and takes joy indifferently,
Lives in the life undying! That which is
Can never cease to be; that which is not
Will not exist. To see this truth of both
Is theirs who part essence from accident,
Substance from shadow. Indestructible,
Learn thou! the Life is, spreading life through all;
It cannot anywhere, by any means,
Be anywise diminished, stayed, or changed.
But for these fleeting frames which it informs
With spirit deathless, endless, infinite,
They perish. Let them perish, Prince! and fight!
He who shall say, 'Lo! I have slain a man!'
He who shall think, 'Lo! I am slain!' those both
Know naught! Life cannot slay. Life is not slain!" [36]

In the framework of Hinduism Arjuna was of the Kshatriya (ruler or warrior) class, one level below the highest class, Brahman (priestly). As a nobleman and warrior it was the dharma (preordained duty) of Arjuna to fight. To refuse to fight would cause his atman to accumulate negative or bad karma, which in turn would simply lengthen his cycle of rebirths. But even though Arjuna is instructed to fight and to kill, he also is told that since this world of time and space is simply maya, possessed of no final meaning, the bodies which he might slay have no final significance. All that truly exists is the World-soul, the Paramatman, and Arjuna's own atman can neither slay other atmans nor itself be destroyed.

Actually, although Gandhi referred often to the Gita and claimed to follow its message for his life, the real source for his teaching of ahimsa, or noninjury, was the atheistic and

[36] *Ibid.*, chap. 2, lines 34-39, 48-64.

dualistic religion known as Jainism. This religion, founded in the sixth century B.C. by Mahavira, has a most stringent prohibition against harming any living creature, no matter how minute. Although there are widespread claims made at present on the part of Hindus that India is a land of peace and of spiritual leadership, as opposed to a West of violence and materialism, much of this contrast is of recent vintage and poorly aged. In the words of A. L. Basham, speaking of Buddhist India in the first millennium A.D.:

War was generally accepted as a normal activity of the state, even by Buddhist kings. The doctrine of non-violence, which in medieval India had become very influential, and had made most of the respectable classes vegetarian, was never at this time taken to forbid war or capital punishment. It was only in modern times that Mahātmā Gāndhī reinterpreted it in this sense.[37]

As with the Golden Rule and the Ten Commandments, the teaching of nonviolence is found in many religions, but its meaning and practical results vary as widely as the circles of faith which profess the teaching.

## The Relation Between Religion and Ethics

It is to be hoped that this discussion of the Golden Rule, the Ten Commandments, and nonviolence in some of the world's religions will serve to document the thesis that it is a mistake to approach the world's religions through the assumed common denominator of ethical living. But, though it might be agreed that the question of the circle of faith within which one thinks and acts is more important than the particular ethical actions which give expression to one's faith, there is yet another aspect of this problem with which we must deal. This problem is raised by the contention that "religion and morality are synonymous." This position was given classic expression in William Ernest Hocking's Hibbert Lectures,

[37] *The Wonder That Was India* (Evergreen ed.; New York: Grove Press, 1959), p. 123.

*Living Religions and a World Faith.* In defining the nature of religion, Professor Hocking states that *"religion is a passion for righteousness, and for the spread of righteousness, conceived as a cosmic demand."* He adds that "Religion is a neighbor of morality, but it is not the same thing." [38] He means by this that true religion is not simply the way of society but must reflect the element of cosmic demand in the deepest sense of man's response.

Although some form of religious observance is found in every society, it is not true that every religion is concerned with high morality. It is closer to the facts to say that no society can exist without minimum laws to restrain the selfish animal passions of man and to maintain some kind of minimum "morality." The very word "morality" comes from the Latin term *mores*, which means "custom," or "the way of the folk." No society can exist without laws against murder, sexual impropriety (as defined by that particular society), or stealing. This is one reason why so many religions, each of which originated in a particular society, have a sort of Ten Commandments. And these minimum laws are borrowed and passed around from culture to culture and even from religion to religion. Paul's ethical teachings, for instance, have much in common both in form and content with the ethical teachings of Stoicism, Hellenistic Judaism, and other religions and philosophies of his day.

Even though all societies have ethical codes, it does not follow that all religions are moral. In the days of Elijah and Hosea we find the prophets of Yahweh opposing the Baal cult. And the literature of the Baal cult which has been uncovered at Ugarit demonstrates that the righteous indignation of the prophets was not misplaced. Wright and Filson point out that the morality of the Canaanites as a society was undoubtedly on a much higher plane than was practiced in the name of the Baal cult. Child sacrifice, sacred prostitution, and

[38] (London: George Allen & Unwin, 1940), p. 26 (author's italics).

drunken debauchery were the frequent practices of this cult.[39]

This lack of high morality, or even the sanctioning of immorality, is found in many other religious communities. The famous Thugs of Hinduism would murder, steal, and practice antisocial sexual rites as part of their service to the goddess Kali. Kali, as the consort of Shiva, the god of destruction, is still served with fanatic devotion in ways that many would label immoral. An interesting example of a religion without morality in the prophetic sense is that of Japanese Shinto. With its teaching that each man is *kami*—that each Japanese contains a portion of divine power—there is no need for ethical teaching, since one who acts naturally will act as a god. In Shinto, what is considered improper conduct is not to be found proscribed in strict codes of law, but rather in prohibitions against breaking tabus, or warnings not to become contaminated with unclean or ritually impure objects. This void in Shinto in the area of ethics was filled from two sources. The first was from Confucianism, including such teachings as filial piety, and the duties involved in the five relationships of life. The other source was Buddhism, from which the famous Bushido code was developed. Yet even this code was basically for the nobility and not for the common people. Shinto morality is first of all based upon obedience to the Japanese emperor and the state; it contains no "passion for righteousness, and for the spread of righteousness" in the sense in which Hocking explains the meaning of righteousness.

*The relation between religion and morality.* Since the content of morality is rooted in society and culture it would appear that there is no real problem in any religion of knowing what is right and what is wrong. As Alan Richardson has reminded us, "all men know that there is a difference between right and wrong." It can be said, without danger of contradiction, that almost every living person in the past twenty-four hours has either thought or done what he knows he should not think or do or has failed to do or think as he knows he

---

[39] Cf., e.g., G. E. Wright and F. V. Filson, eds., *The Westminster Historical Atlas to the Bible* (Philadelphia: The Westminster Press, 1945), p. 36.

should. The real problem of morality is that of motivation, of the sanctions for one's actions. And that is one of the functions of religion. But it is possible for religion, as a motivating force, to sanction a morality which is below the level of the society in which it is found, to identify the accepted morality of the day with the religion, or in some few cases to call society to a higher level of conduct.

We have noted instances where religion lends aid to the debauching of society as in the Old Testament Baal cult or among the Thugs of India. In other instances it is difficult to discern a clear line between a religion and its traditional culture, as is true for much of Hinduism and traditional Judaism. But in some ways it is possible to interpret the ethical teachings of such great leaders as the Buddha, Confucius, Moses, Socrates, Jesus, and Muhammad as calling upon men to rise above the morality of their culture. The absolute imperatives of Gautama and Jesus represent both a condemnation of the usual ways of men and a challenge to follow an absolute ethic. Although this could be illustrated by quotations from each of these men, the words of Jesus are most familiar: "You have heard that it was said, 'You shall not commit adultery.' But I say to you that everyone who looks at a woman lustfully has already committed adultery with her in his heart." [40]

In any religion faith precedes works. In any religion the reason why one believes he should or should not do certain things is based upon his circle of faith. It is a great temptation to seize upon the element of ethical concern as a common denominator in the world's religions. Yet if two systems such as Christianity and communism, or Christianity and Buddhism, are measured and compared by the ethical test without regard for underlying beliefs, the conclusions arrived at could be completely misleading. In fact, such a test might be irrelevant to a given religion and simply reflect the prejudice of the one so judging.

[40] Matt. 5:27-28.

CHAPTER 5

# O MASTER, LET ME
# WALK WITH THEE!

This chapter continues the discussion of our thesis of *circles of faith* by means of a rapid study of four of the great religious leaders of history. In chronological order these are: Gautama, the Buddha; Confucius, the Chinese sage; Jesus, the Christ; and Muhammad, the Messenger of Allah. Each of these men has had hundreds of millions of followers, and each has been and remains a controversial figure. This is true not only within each religion—witness merely the large number of Christian sects and movements—but also for the secular historians who seek to interpret their lives and careers.

It is possible to tell the story of mankind from the perspective of the contribution of its leaders, and no study of history has much appeal without a strong emphasis upon this aspect of the human drama. Yet the giants of history baffle analysis, and one can read a dozen lives of Napoleon or Lincoln without actually solving the mystery of the tremendous power each possessed as a leader of men. Not only do the contributions of such leaders elude final analysis, it also is not possible to offer an unbiased account of their lives and influence. The point of view of the writer, the silences of history, the un-
112

critical nature of our sources, to say nothing of the cursory nature of this chapter, necessarily distort the evaluation of the career of each of these men. For such reasons a descriptive theory of leadership will be employed to present each man in terms of his career as a religious leader and thus to facilitate a discussion of the varied nature of the appeal each has to the loyalty of his followers.

*The conjuncture hypothesis of leadership.* There is a theory which attempts to explain or describe the phenomenon of leadership by means of three factors which are always associated with the act of leading.[1] The first of these factors is the historical context in which the people are in need of a leader and which makes his leadership both necessary and possible. This includes the social, economic, and political situation of his day and the values and needs of the people who are led. The second factor is the leader himself—his personality, his abilities, and his experience and training which fit him for leadership. The final factor is that of an event, or events, intruding into the life of the leader making his leadership possible. To the secular historian this usually would be a natural event such as the untimely death of King George VI of England which placed Elizabeth II on the throne. In this case, as would be true in most instances of leadership, other events beyond the control of Queen Elizabeth should also be included, such as her royal birth, and the unprecedented abdication of her uncle which placed her in direct line to the accession.

If each of these three factors of the historical situation, the leader, and the key event which intrudes into the leader's life is in proper alignment, in conjunction with one another, then we have a description of leadership known as "the conjuncture hypothesis of leadership." That is, leadership may be described in terms of an analysis of these three factors and their coincidence. Let us illustrate this hypothesis. Winston Churchill, in 1939, was a man of proved ability in several fields. The times

---

[1] Clarence Marsh Case, "Leadership and Conjuncture, A Sociological Hypothesis," *Sociology and Social Research*, 6:510-513 (July-August, 1933).

cried for strong leadership. Yet Churchill was already tapering off his career into retirement, and it was only the event of the start of World War II and concomitant events which made possible his leadership in wartime England. Turning to Russia for another example, we find that in 1917, when the social situation demanded leadership, Lenin was a well-known revolutionary and Marxist author but with no power or following. The events of the defeat of Czarist Russia by Germany and the initial attempt at revolution, with its resultant chaos, made possible the Bolshevist seizure of power, and thereby, Lenin's leadership of the Soviet Republic.

Illustrations could easily be multiplied, but the decisive factor in this descriptive hypothesis of the phenomenon of leadership is that of the event. Obviously both the times and the man who leads must be included in any description of leadership. But it also is essential to any explanation of a leader's influence to seek out the event or series of events which intrude into history and the leader's career to make his leadership possible, and to realize that all must conjoin to produce the phenomenon of leadership.

There is, however, yet another dimension to the problem which is of central importance. It is now a truism to state that all interpretations of history remain subjective and that one reading of a leader's accomplishments might be diametrically opposite to that of another. Imagine the differences in interpretation possible between the autobiography of Adolf Hitler and his biography as written by an exiled German Jew, or the late Winston Churchill.

This problem of interpretation and evaluation appears to be especially difficult in the area of religion. This is for such reasons as are linked with any attempt to understand the leadership of a person such as Adolf Hitler. Fanatical loyalty and blind hate were felt by persons on different sides of the German struggle, and to this day there are those who cannot understand how Germany could have produced a leader such as Hitler. When one turns to consider religious leaders such as Gautama or Jesus this factor of faith is even more important, and it clearly divides those who believe in the leader from those outside the circle of the religion. A well-known Buddhist author states that "Gautama the Buddha was the Buddha because he was *Buddha*, the Enlightened One, and he who cannot accept this premise will never know more than the shell of Buddhism." [2] This statement of faith by a devout Buddhist can be paralleled with similar confessions by the followers of other great religious leaders. Thus, the apostle Paul tells the Corinthian Christians that "no one can say 'Jesus is Lord' except by the Holy Spirit." [3] Again, to the Muslim, Muhammad is the *Rasul*, or the messenger *par excellence*, of Allah. For the past 2,500 years Confucius has been regarded by most Chinese as the true Sage whose character and way are to be emulated if one is to find meaning and fulfillment for his life.

This further dimension of faith in the evaluation of a religious leader actually is the decisive factor in the Buddhist's view of the Buddha or in what the Christian thinks about Christ. The day is past when the secular, so-called objective historian can claim to present a fair, accurate, and unbiased portrait of such a man as Gautama or Muhammad. Biblical scholars long since have achieved a major victory in this respect. An atheist or a secular historian is able to describe, quite clearly, the events, contents, and obvious meanings of the New Testament drama. But this does not mean that he is unbiased nor that he understands the inner meaning of the drama as it affects the personal lives of believing Christians. It is now axiomatic that the Christian scholar may be better qualified than the atheistic or secular historian to describe and explain New Testament events, simply because the Christian is able to combine the most critical methods with sympathetic understanding. From my perspective as a Christian I will here try to describe the careers of Gautama, Confucius, Jesus, and Muhammad, and to include in each statement the decisive at-

[2] Humphreys, *Buddhism*, p. 25.
[3] I Cor. 12:3.

titude of faith of the followers, even though this must of necessity be the most faulty aspect of the analysis.

## Gautama, the Buddha

The life and teachings of the man who is revered as the Buddha by hundreds of millions of people in South and East Asia are known to us almost entirely through legend and myth. We have nothing such as the Christian Gospel record about Jesus to help us in recovering the story of the founder of Buddhism. We are not even sure of his dates, but Buddhist tradition fixes his birth in 544 B.C., and Western scholarship about 567 B.C. The tradition tells us that he lived about eighty years.

Although it can be misleading to compare the beginnings of Buddhism to those of Christianity, it can also be helpful. Christianity arose as a Jewish sectarian movement and, as we know from such evidence as the Dead Sea Scrolls, for some time was simply one of several similar Jewish sects, competing with its message of salvation, and seeking followers to strengthen the emerging Christian churches. Buddhism, in a similar vein, had its origins in the Hinduism of India of the sixth century B.C. It also was but one of several sectarian movements offering new solutions to the religious and social problems of that day. For by this time the fairly simple society of the Aryan invaders (c. 1500-1000 B.C.), with its cult of ancestors and gods of nature, had become quite complex. A. L. Basham characterizes the sixth century B.C. in India as a time "of great social change, when old tribal units were breaking up. The feeling of group solidarity which the tribe gave was removed, and men stood face to face with the world, with no refuge in their kinsmen. Chieftains were overthrown, their courts dispersed, their lands and tribesmen absorbed in the greater kingdoms. A new order was coming into being." [4]

The religious situation was characterized by the dominance of the Brahman, or priestly, class. In earlier Vedic times the

[4] *The Wonder That Was India* p. 246.

highest class had been the Kshatriya, the warrior or ruling class. This group at first had functioned both as a priestly and ruling class, much as the Hebrew patriarch Abraham in Genesis was both priest and political leader before the rise of the Levitical priesthood. But over the centuries the developing complexities of the sacrifices and rituals, and a hardening legalism, made the expert in religious lore and rites the one who controlled the means of salvation. Knowledge of the Vedas, and the accompanying sacrifices with which the sacred verses were chanted, was primarily in the possession of the Brahmans. The dogma was gaining acceptance that only members of this highest Brahman class could be sure of death-less peace at the end of this present life. Members of the other three classes—the Kshatriya, Vaisya, and Shudra—were believed to be doomed to one or more further earthly existences before they could obtain *moksha*, or release, from the cycle of births and deaths in which all men were believed to be enmeshed. This priestly domination had helped create conditions for reform which call to mind the situation in Europe in Martin Luther's day.

One important challenge to Brahmanism is reflected in the philosophical monism of the *Upanishads* which flourished in this period and which a bit later was to become the basis of the classical Hindu world view. This is known as *jnana-marga*, the way of salvation by knowledge.[5] There were those who were willing and able to meet the demands of world denial and meditation which were prerequisite to this way of liberation. For these the goal of religious striving was to realize the identity of one's *atman* (soul) with the *Paramatman* (World-soul) and thereby to anticipate union with the World-soul at death. From the clan and family names of persons who participated in the dialogues of the Upanishads we know that many were members of the Kshatriya class. Even though this way of salvation meant that liberation need not be re-

[5] See above, pp. 70-73.

stricted to the Brahman class it was a lonely way which never attracted a large following.

It was into the Kshatriya class that Siddhartha Gautama was born. His father was a chieftain of a small city-state in northeast India, just south of modern Nepal. Historians agree that young Gautama married and had one son, Rahula. At about the age of thirty he left his wife and infant child, renounced his right to inherit his father's rule, and joined the ranks of mendicant Hindu holy men to seek his salvation. We are told that for six years he followed strenuously the accepted paths to salvation of that day. He first studied the current philosophical systems and surpassed all his teachers in learning. Unsatisfied, he turned to the way of bodily discipline and again surpassed his teachers in practice of the ascetic life, attracting five close disciples in the process. He became a living skeleton, so total was his abstinence, but this too failed to satisfy his search. Finally he seated himself under a tree and vowed not to move from his place until he had attained his goal.

At this point Gautama experienced what is called the "Great Awakening" (bodhi) and attained buddhahood, the condition of being fully enlightened. He now was the Buddha, the "enlightened one." In chapter three[6] we summarized the Buddha's message of salvation, so here we will recount only the essential details. These usually are summarized as the Four Holy Truths and affirm that human existence is to be equated with dukkha, or suffering (that to exist is to suffer), and that suffering, and existence, are caused by tanha, craving or desire. His message of hope was that tanha can be eliminated, and that this is possible if one follows the Noble Eightfold Path. When one thus eliminates desire he also will eliminate suffering and at death bring an end to the cycle of births into this world. He would experience the bliss of nirvana in this life and also enter into this blessed state at death. The purpose of following the Noble Eightfold Path, therefore, is to enable

[6] See above, pp. 76-80.

one to cease to exist as a self. That is, the Buddha taught that to exist is to suffer, but that the end of the path of the Buddha is nirvana, or the waning away of the self.

Having found this way of release or peace, of nirvana or the "blowing out" of the flames of desires which cause birth, sorrow, and suffering, Gautama began to preach his doctrine to his ascetic friends and then to any who would listen. The new teaching quickly attracted followers and spread rapidly, partly because of the good news that all men, not just Brahmans, could achieve cessation of rebirth in this present life. Along with the preaching of this way of salvation was taught a body of moral discipline which served to guide the convert in his new life.

Gautama taught his message and led his new movement for some forty-five years after his enlightenment. During this time he founded an order (*Sangha*) of monks and later one for nuns. Whoever joined the order was called upon to renounce completely his past way of life—family, job, position in the community—and to live as a beggar without possessions or any other attachment to the world. By the time of Gautama's death the movement had spread over much of India and had many thousands of members, and there were even more lay followers who supported the movement with gifts of money, food, and land. These lay followers represented those who were unwilling, in this present existence, to make the sacrifice of becoming a mendicant *bhikku*. Thus Buddhism soon became a religion distinct from the Hinduism out of which it had sprung. Today there are scores of millions of Buddhists spread from Ceylon to Japan, and many hundreds of millions more whose lives are directly influenced by the world view of Buddhism.

It is an obvious fact of history that Gautama, the man, had a message that appealed to his followers. The times called for a leader and his message met that need. According to the conjuncture hypothesis of leadership outlined above, however, there must also be some key event which accounts for the specific success of Gautama as the founder of this new religion.

Although we have real difficulty in answering historical questions about Buddha, many Western historians take the position that a key factor in explaining Gautama's burning quest and his dramatic success was that of his birth into the Kshatriya, the second or warrior class of Hinduism. As a member of this class he would be, by Brahmanical standards, denied any hope of achieving release from the cycle of death and rebirth at the end of his present existence. Instead he was fated to be reborn one or more times until he would be reborn as a member of the highest, Brahman, class.

Following this possibility, the historian argues that Gautama, denied the orthodox way of salvation, sought another way that might be open to him and to all other men as well. Although he might have found salvation as a Kshatriya by following the way of knowledge, he is reported to have rejected this approach. Instead he taught the Four Noble Truths as a way open to all. From this premise it could be argued that if Gautama had not been born into the Kshatriya class it is quite probable that Buddhism would not have been born.

The Buddhist views the life, enlightenment, and ministry of Buddha from an entirely different point of view. He does not even start with the same view of history that the Westerner has, nor would the theory of leadership which we are exploring have much appeal to him as an approach to understanding his Master. For him it is not the Buddha's human birth as Kshatriya that is significant, although this is not ignored in the tradition. The central event, the all-important fact of Gautama's life is that of his Enlightenment. But this must be understood in a much different circle of faith than that of Western rationalism. Although most would agree that the Enlightenment was the real beginning of Buddhism, all too often the meaning of Gautama's experience is reduced to current psychological terms which, for a Buddhist, runs the danger of substituting mere description for its actual meaning. Of course we are long past the day of such a flat statement as that of W. R. Van Buskirk in *Saviors of Mankind*,[7] when he

[7] (New York: The Macmillan Company, 1929) p. 92.

says that the Buddha "had thought his system through." Yet we find, in the book currently used most widely as a text in courses in world religions, written by one who is both a model of fairness and a practitioner of the historical method, the following description of this event.

The Buddhist books insist that he set his teeth and said to himself determinedly: "Though skin, nerves, and bone shall waste away, and life-blood itself be dried up, here sit I till I attain Enlightenment." In all probability the fact was far otherwise; psychology probably can suggest a truer version of the real course of Gautama's enlightenment: he had tried too hard altogether, so that his very determination stood between him and the state of consciousness which he desired; but now, in the face of self-defeat, his will relaxed, he let his mind wander back over his previous experience. Some such questions as these must have arisen in his mind: What was he to think of his life and his search for salvation until now? Why had he failed?

And suddenly the answer came. The stumbling-block to his own salvation, and the cause of all human misery, he reasoned, was desire—too intense desire (tanha, "thirst," "craving,")—desire for the wrong things, arising out of the carnal will-to-live-and-have. The intensity of his own desire had defeated him.[8]

The question arises, is Professor Noss here talking about the Buddha's enlightenment, or is he offering a psychological explanation for Western ears which parades as an objective and, therefore, true explanation of what "really" happened? My concern here is not to disagree with Noss, because I find myself in the same camp simply by going through the process of this chapter. What I am suggesting is this: To attempt to be objective, to seek truth wherever it may be found, should never be permitted to blind us to the fact that, especially in the field of religion, we may be leaving out an entire dimension of understanding. Difficult, even impossible, though it may be, we must make the attempt to view an event such as this in

[8] John B. Noss, Man's Religions (3rd ed.; New York: The Macmillan Company, 1963), p. 174.

121

terms of what it might have meant, and continues to mean, to men of Buddhist faith.

For the Buddhist, then, the conviction that Gautama truly was the Enlightened One is not simply a historical item— "One day, Gautama, sitting under the Bo tree thought through his system." To a man of Buddhist faith the Enlightenment means, at the least, that after many, perhaps thousands of earthly (and heavenly) existences, the One reborn as Gautama, who had purified himself for this supreme achievement with rigorous endeavor through all of those lives, finally had broken the bonds which held him to the stream of life. And he who had thus trod the path to the cessation of rebirths, in his infinite compassion, chose to postpone entering the nirvana which he had won so arduously that he might teach to others the Way which he had found. Unfortunately, this description also, like that of Professor Noss, consists merely of English words addressed to readers, of whom most do not believe in karma, or rebirth. Let us, therefore, cite an example from Buddhist literature to indicate a bit of the mystery and the glory which surrounds a Buddhist understanding of the Enlightenment. Sir Edwin Arnold, in his rendering of the life of the Buddha called *The Light of Asia*, tells how the Buddha, "in hearing of all Times and Worlds," spoke as follows:

> Many a House of Life
> Hath held me—seeking ever him who wrought
> These prisons of the senses, sorrow-fraught;
> Sore was my ceaseless strife!
>
> But now,
> Thou Builder of this Tabernacle—Thou!
> I know Thee! Never shalt thou build again
> These walls of pain,
> Nor raise the roof-tree of deceits, nor lay
> Fresh rafters on the clay;
> Broken thy house is, and the ridge-pole split!
> Delusion fashioned it!
> Safe pass I thence—deliverance to obtain.[9]

* End of Book VI.

Let us use one more illustration, this time from *Gautama: The Story of the Lord Buddha*, as told by Shakuntala Masani. The Buddha, seated under the Bo tree, has just arrived at "the four great truths which were the Law of the Wheel of Life." We then read of cosmic reactions to this great event:

When these divine truths were revealed to the Lord all the worlds quaked with a terrible violence, and the words, "Most excellent Being, the Divine Buddha," resounded throughout the Universe. Gorgeous flags and banners were unfolded in the heavens, and wonderful ornaments decorated the skies as the divine spirits celebrated the hope of their own salvation. A celestial light shone through the sky and illuminated all things. Its rays pentrated to hell's darkest abyss. All was Light.[10]

It is in the context of reverence such as this for the Buddha, and belief in the cosmic meaning of his career, that the dictum of Christmas Humphreys given earlier in this chapter is to be understood: "Gautama the Buddha was the Buddha because he was *Buddha*, the Enlightened One, and he who cannot accept this premise will never know more than the shell of Buddhism." It is almost impossible for one who is not a believer to know what it means to follow the Buddha as one's master and to tread the path which he trod. Miss I. B. Horner describes the Buddha after his Enlightenment in paradoxical language, as one who, although he was

incomputable after the attainment of Buddhahood, and was not to be reckoned by any of the aggregates (*khandā*) as the constituents of the living body and mind came to be called . . . , he was in no way hidden from human sight while he was alive. He was a man in a human body, not a phantom of Glory become apparent to men, far less a god or a mythological figure.[11]

The many titles bestowed on Gautama as the Buddha also attest to the reverence held for him. He is Sakya-Muni, "sage

[10] (New York: The Macmillan Company, 1956) p. 61.
[11] In Zaehner, *The Concise Encyclopedia of Living Faiths*, p. 282.

of the Sakyas"—the tribe from which he was descended; he is called Tathāgata, an untranslatable title, but which means something like "he who is thus gone," or one who has attained; *Bhagavan*, or Lord, a term also used for the Hindu God, Krishna. These and many other titles are used, much as Christians have scores of titles for Jesus as risen Lord and Christ. But beyond this phenomenon lie the many legends and myths which are woven into the story of the Buddha. Not only was he of miraculous birth, but he was one who performed great miracles, and who was omniscient; there also is a whole cycle of stories, called *Jataka* tales, told about the Buddha's previous existences when he was perfecting himself for his final birth. And just as he was foreordained to become Enlightened and many marvels attended his birth, his father is transformed from a petty chieftan into a magnificent ruler whose attempts to keep his son from renouncing the world are frustrated by the gods. Once Gautama is regarded as the Buddha one finds that almost anything in the world of gods and of men may be ascribed to him, since he is truly the Tathāgata.[12]

### Master K'ung, the Sage of China

Although Confucius has had almost no following outside the Chinese people and is a somewhat controversial subject to historians of religions insofar as he is claimed as a religious leader, he represents a different circle of faith for our purposes than do other founders such as Mahavira (Jainism), Zoroaster (Parsis), and Nanak (the Sikhs). Because of this, and also because Confucianism has had a tremendous influence throughout East Asia, especially in Japan, the life, career, and influence of Confucius will be considered in terms of the conjuncture hypothesis in order that we might compare and contrast his leadership with that of Gautama, Jesus, and Muhammad.

As is true for the Buddha, it is difficult to sort out the Con-

---

[12] Cf. F. H. Hilliard, *The Buddha, the Prophet and the Christ* (New York: The Macmillan Company, 1956) for ways in which each of these men was honored in tradition and legend.

fucius of history from the traditions and legends surrounding him. He lived in the latter part of the long Chou dynasty (1122-249 B.C.), his traditional dates being 551-479 B.C. He lived in East Central China in what is today Shantung and Honan provinces. As appears to be so often the case with great leaders, the times in which he lived were chaotic, and ideas and movements were in ferment. It was a feudal age, long before China was unified under the Emperor Shi-Huang-Ti (221-207 B.C.), a period marked by constant wars between the many Chinese states, and by invasions by barbarians. Chinese religion at this time consisted essentially of nature and ancestor worship, although the abstract concept of *Tao* was employed to refer to the cosmic way of nature, and the terms *Shang Ti* (exalted ancestor) and *t'ien* (heaven) were used to refer to a sort of sky-god. But as was indicated earlier in chapter three,[13] Confucius' first concern was not in the area of religious reform but in that of human relations.

We know about him from several sources, notably the Analects, or "Discourses" which recount anecdotes about his life preserved by his disciples and followers; a treatise known as the *Chung Yung* (Doctrine of the Mean or Central Harmony) ascribed to his grandson, Tsu Ssu; and a second-century B.C. biography by Ssu Ma Ch'ien, included in his history of China. He was apparently of illegitimate birth and was raised by his mother who was able to provide him with an education. He married at about nineteen and had a daughter and a son. After divorcing his wife he supported himself for years either as a menial laborer or as a teacher—the tradition is both uncertain and unreliable—and then for some time in administrative work in local government. At about the age of fifty, according to the tradition, he was invited by the duke of his home state of Lu to serve as administrative ruler of the dukedom. Confucius was thus afforded an opportunity to put into practice his theories of government and to institute social and moral reform. He is reported to have been so successful that a neighboring ruler became envious and con-

[13] See above, pp. 81-82.

cerned lest Confucius' management make the Duke of Lu too successful. Legend then recounts how this envious ruler turned the heart of the Duke from virtue with a gift of dancing girls and race horses, with the result that Confucius resigned his post in protest.

After this discouraging experience Confucius, accompanied by a few close disciples, wandered from province to province for some ten years, offering his services as administrator to any ruler who was willing to accept his exacting conditions. He refused some offers of employment and appears never to have found a ruler who was willing to accept the challenge to aspire to the ideal of the sage-king.

Confucius finally decided to abandon his quest, and he returned to his home province where he spent his last few years on two main projects. The first was the editing of the ancient classics which he felt contained the record of the true way of life for man and for society. The second was the establishment of a school for those young men who were willing to study hard and were open to instruction. The classical writings which he selected and edited were used as the basic curriculum for Confucius' school since he was convinced that they held the key to the problems of man and society. The system of instruction which he developed and the scholarly tradition which he established survived him and were to become the basis for Confucianism as a school of thought. This is known in China as the Ju Chiao (pronounced roo jow), the School of the Scholar.

Confucius' biographer tells of how, during the last illness of the Sage, when his disciple, Tsekung, came to visit him Confucius reproached him with the words,

"Ah Sze, why do you turn up so late?" Confucius then sighed and sang a song:

> "Ah! the [great mountain] is crumbling down!
> The pillar is falling down!
> The philosopher is passing out!"

He then shed tears and spoke to Tsekung. "For a long time the world has been living in moral chaos, and no ruler has been able to follow me . . . ." Seven days afterwards he died, aged seventy-three. This was on the day chich'ou of April, in the sixteenth year of Duke Ai.[14]

After a brief summary of Confucius' life such as has just been given H. G. Creel says: "His life had about it very little of the dramatic. There was no climax and no martyrdom. None of his chief ambitions had been fulfilled. There is little doubt that when he died everyone considered him a failure. Certainly he himself did." [15]

But, as Creel goes on to point out, Confucius' influence did survive him and slowly but surely the "School of the Scholar" gained the ascendance over the "one hundred schools," and for over two thousand years, up to the Communist era beginning in 1949, Confucianism was the dominant tradition in China. The Analects were compiled by his disciples, his grandson wrote the *Central Harmony*, which gave a systematic and sympathetic treatment of Confucius' basic teachings, and he was memorialized in the biography by the historian Ssu Ma Ch'ien. For a short while, toward the end of the third century B.C., a total eclipse of the movement threatened. During the short-lived reign of Shi-Huang-Ti, who invaded the central part of China from the northwest, unified China, and established the Ch'in dynasty, Confucianism came under attack as reactionary, and all books stressing the way of the ancients were ordered burned.

But the effects of this disaster were quickly reversed in the Han dynasty (202 B.C.-A.D. 220) and toward the end of this period certain texts attribute omniscience, and even omnipotence, to Confucius.[16] To skip quickly through the centuries, in the twelfth century the neo-Confucianist movement utilized the name and influence of the indigenous philosopher to construct a system to offset the foreign Buddhist philosophy

[14] Lin Yutang, *The Wisdom of Confucius*, pp. 96-97.
[15] *Confucius: the Man and the Myth* (New York: The John Day Company, 1949), p. 3.
[16] Cf. Wing-tsit Chan, *Religious Trends in Modern China* (New York: Columbia University Press, 1953), p. 5.

and cosmology. Both Confucianism, and aspects of neo-Confucianism, continued to be major influences in intellectual, social, and political life right into the twentieth century. In 1906 the Dowager Empress of the dying Manchu dynasty ordered Confucius to be sacrificed to as a god; President Sun Yat Sen of the Chinese Republic utilized the Confucian principles to undergird his New Life Movement, and finally, Chiang Kai Shek did the same in the 1930's.[17] Today, even though under the Communists Confucianism as a state religion is dead, one can agree with Wing-tsit Chan that it is, and will continue to be for a long time, an important part of the thought and way of life of the Chinese people.[18]

In chapter three we summarized the basic message of salvation which Confucius proclaimed. He assumed that in the golden age of ancient China there had existed a true nobility, and that all the people at that time had lived in harmony because the rulers were kind and just and the people were industrious and obedient. He believed that the reason there were chaos and war, famine, and family strife in his day was because the ancient ways were neglected. The nobility were such in name only, while the common people, who were aware of this, had lost all respect for law and order. Confucius' solution was quite simple. He maintained that true nobility was not a matter of birth, but of inner character. By proper education and training in the ancient ways men could be taught to live by the five virtues and evidence true nobility by their inner character. Thus he sought to produce a group of chün tzu, "noblemen," who would in turn be able to create an ideal society wherein everyone knew his proper role in life and performed the duty which corresponded to his social station. When we search for the event, the third factor in our conjuncture hypothesis of leadership which helps us describe Confucius' leadership, it would appear that it was the fact that Confucius was born of common stock. Just as Gautama,

[17] Ibid., p. 24.
[18] Ibid., p. 53.

born into the Kshatriya class, sought a way of salvation which did not require birth into the higher Brahman class, so Confucius taught that one did not become a "gentleman" or chün tzu by birth, but only by proper education and virtuous living. This was, of course, a revolutionary principle, because its implication was that anyone (including Confucius) could become a gentleman and that birth was no longer important.

A second event intruding into Confucius' career which helps us account for his ultimate success as a leader was, ironically, the series of failures in his life's work: his failure to have the Duke of Lu be single-hearted in his government of the province, which led to Confucius' resignation as administrator; his failure during his years of wandering to find a single ruler willing to follow his way; and the end of his life, when he was preceded in death by at least two disciples in whom he had placed high hopes to carry on his work, and his own death with no clear prospect that any of his teaching would survive.

It is not possible to unravel the curtain of history at this point and determine just why Confucius, the apparent failure, became the most important single individual to appear in the tradition of the world's oldest continuous culture. Perhaps Confucius' single-minded devotion to his conviction that he had the mandate of t'ien, and his refusal to compromise or deviate from his understanding of the Way of Heaven, were sufficient motivation to his disciples and later followers to ensure that his teaching would be continued. Recent Western scholarship has properly been reassessing the appraisement of Confucius given by several generations of Christian missionaries. Far from viewing him as a "stuffed shirt" whose interests lay in a reactionary recovering of the dead past, or in "face-saving" formal manners, authors such as Arthur Waley, George Herbert Kenney, and H. G. Creel have been helping us see a different Confucius who is much more creditable in terms of his positive influence on Chinese history and culture. In the words of Creel:

He is often called a reactionary, whose primary aim was to restore the ways of antiquity and to bolster the authority of the hereditary aristocracy. In fact, he advocated and helped to bring about such sweeping social and political reforms that he must be counted among the great revolutionaries. Within a few centuries after his death hereditary aristocracy had virtually ceased to exist in China, and Confucius had contributed more than any other man to its destruction.[19]

To the Confucian follower—the Confucian man of faith, if you will—he was the Perfect Sage. In the *Central Harmony*, ascribed to his grandson, we cannot be sure when Confucius is the subject and when the reference is to the ideal Sage, but certainly in the mind of the Confucianist they are fused. Even in the humanistic translation of Lin Yutang the adulation of Confucius shines through:

Oh, how great is the divine moral law of the Sage. Overflowing and illimitable, it gives birth and life to all created things and towers high up to the very heavens. How magnificent it is! How imposing the three hundred principles and three thousand rules of conduct! . . .

Wherefore it is that it is true of the really great moral man that every move he makes becomes an example for generations; every act he does becomes a model for generations and every word he utters becomes a guide for generations. Those who are far away look up to him, while those who are near do not decrease their respect for him. In the *Book of Songs* it is said:

"There they found no fault of him,
Here they never tire of him;
Thus from day to day and night to night
They will perpetuate his praise!" [20]

We read in the biography by Ssu Ma Ch'ien that Confucius was nine feet six inches tall.[21] Many commentators

[19] *Confucius*, p. 1.
[20] *The Wisdom of Confucius*, p. 126, 129.
[21] *Ibid.*, p. 57.

hasten to point out that the measurement of feet in those days was much less than now. Perhaps this is true, but when I read this passage I am reminded that to the Confucian his master was, in our contemporary phrase, "ten feet tall."

## Jesus, the Christ

Whole libraries have been written about Jesus of Nazareth, and there is no need to add to the debate which has continued through the centuries about the person of Christ. But in order to continue the use of our pattern of the theory of leadership which has been applied to Gautama and Confucius we will first recount Jesus' career from the point of view of descriptive history, and then attempt to isolate that event which makes Jesus unique for the Christian.

We actually know more about the Judaism of Jesus' day than we do about the life of Jesus itself. The Jews long had cherished the hope that someday God would come to the aid of his people and restore them to a place of importance among the nations. Yet in first-century Palestine the Romans ruled with an iron hand. The series of puppet kings and Roman governors were constant reminders of foreign government and pagan domination. The Jews were taxed mercilessly for the benefit of the Empire, and it appeared as though Yahweh had forgotten his chosen people. Though many of the pious sought to obey God's will as revealed in his Law the future looked bleak.

Such New Testament scholars as Albert Schweitzer, Charles Guignebert, Maurice Goguel, Rudolf Bultmann, and many others have labored diligently to recover the historical Jesus, insofar as it is possible with the available records. What little we do know about his life has been summed up by John Knox in his book, *The Man Christ Jesus*. The following biographical data, he affirms, are to be considered established.

We can say such things, for example, as that he was born in Palestine during the reign of Herod the Great; that he was brought up

131

in Nazareth; that he lived the normal life of a Jew of his period
and locale; that he was baptized by John, a proclaimer of the early
coming of God's judgment; that he spent a year or more in teaching, somewhat in the manner of contemporary rabbis, groups of
his fellow countrymen in various parts of Palestine, mostly in
Galilee, and in more intimate association with some chosen
friends and disciples; that he incurred the hostility of some of his
compatriots and the suspicion of the Roman authorities; that he
was put to death in Jerusalem by these same authorities during
the procuratorship of Pilate.[22]

The historian would go on to speculate that Jesus was a
Jewish prophet much like his immediate predecessor, John the
Baptist. John had proclaimed the imminent coming of God's
kingdom and had instituted the rite of baptism to purify his
followers in preparation for this cosmic event. He baptized
Jesus and soon after was arrested. Perhaps it was John's ar-
rest, along with the obvious plight of the Jewish people, which
convinced Jesus that God could not long delay intervening
in the affairs of his people. With this burning conviction
Jesus, like John, proclaimed that God's kingdom or rule was
about to be inaugurated. Since this implied that all earthly
rule would be overthrown, Jesus was branded a revolutionary,
as one opposed to the Roman rule. Thus a good man was sent
to his death firmly believing in his message and trusting that
God would vindicate him. From the standpoint of history,
therefore, it makes sense to assume that Jesus' death was the
event which caused him to become the founder of a new
religion. Although his followers temporarily forsook his cause,
they soon rallied around the realization of the truth that,
just as Jesus had gone to his death trusting in the God of
Abraham, Moses, and the prophets, they should also be true
to God's demands. Thus they kept the memory of Jesus alive
and even began to claim that he had been raised from the
dead—just as it was rumored during Jesus' ministry that John

[22] (Chicago: Willett, Clark & Company, 1941) pp. 20-21.

the Baptist had been raised from the dead after his execution by Herod Antipas.[23]

But this is not all. Continuing our reconstruction by Western historians, the Christian movement spread rapidly through the Mediterranean world because there already existed many cults of gods who had died and risen from the dead, as well as mystery religions whose members considered themselves to be slaves devoted to their god as lord of their lives, one who would save them from death itself. In the first few decades of Christianity Jesus was represented as one of those dying and rising gods to whose authority the Christian should submit as a slave to his lord. One reason the Christian movement won out over the competing religions of salvation in the Hellenestic world was that Jesus was a real man and not a mythical being such as Dionysius, or the goddess Isis. This potent mixture of Jewish monotheism and Hellenistic savior cult was unbeatable. Thus Jesus' memory produced a viable religion which has survived to this day. The secular historian would claim that Christianity can be studied in terms of its origins, and that the many factors accounting for its growth and survival all lend themselves to a natural description and explanation.

But for the believing Christian this is not sufficient to account for the meaning and influence of Jesus as the Christ and risen Lord. It is true that Jesus' death was a tragic event and Good Friday is an important holy day. The earliest tradition, however, placed emphasis on the fact that God had raised Jesus from the dead, and thereby designated him as the Jewish Messiah (Christ). In the words of the apostle Paul in his letter to the Romans, the gospel which he proclaimed concerned God's "Son, who was descended from David according to the flesh and designated Son of God in power according to the Spirit of holiness by his resurrection from the dead, Jesus Christ our Lord." [24] Professor C. H. Dodd has taught us to

[23] Cf., e.g., Mark 8:28.
[24] Rom. 1:3-4.

refer to this early Christian message as the *kerygma*, or "proclamation" of the good news concerning God's action in history for the salvation of all Christian believers.[25] This raising of Jesus was the culmination of the drama of salvation, of the fulfillment of God's purpose in history which had begun with his promise to Abraham, or, rather, with the very creation of the world and of man. All the events of Jesus' life were part of God's final revelation to the world.

The New Testament was written by believing Christians, after the event of the Resurrection, so that it is only natural to find that the man Jesus and the risen and glorified Christ (Messiah) are so combined, or even made identical, that it is a false approach for the Christian to try to separate the historical Jesus from the Christ of faith. When a man of faith reads in the Gospel of Mark stories about Jesus in which he fed five thousand people with five loaves of bread and two fish,[26] later on fed four thousand people with seven loaves,[27] reads also how Jesus stilled a storm,[28] or walked on the water,[29] or raised Jairus' daughter from the dead,[30] and performed many other miraculous deeds,[31] he is of course reading about his risen Lord who is also Lord of his life and of all creation. This is part of what the anonymous author of the Letter to the Hebrews meant in his prefatory remarks:

"In many and various ways God spoke of old to our fathers by the prophets; but in these last days he has spoken to us by a Son, whom he appointed the heir of all things, through whom also he created the world. He reflects the glory of God and bears the very stamp of his nature, upholding the universe by his word of power." [32]

[25] *The Apostolic Preaching* (New York: Harper & Row, 1937).
[26] Mark 6:30-44.
[27] Mark 8:1-10.
[28] Mark 4:35-41.
[29] Mark 6:45-52.
[30] Mark 5:21-24; 35-43.
[31] Cf., e.g., Alan Richardson, *The Miracle-Stories of the Gospels* (London: SCM Press, 1960).
[32] Heb. 1:1-3.

As with the Buddha, many legends and myths have grown about the story of Jesus, but they all are better understood if they are approached from the perspective of the resurrection faith, from within the Christian circle of faith that assumes all of life to be part of God's miracle of creation. In the Gospel of John the apostle Thomas, called the Twin, when he was told that some of the disciples had seen the risen Lord, said: "Unless I see in his hands the print of the nails, and place my finger in the mark of the nails, and place my hand in his side, I will not believe." In the same story Jesus said to Thomas: "Put out your hand, and place it in my side; do not be faithless, but believing." It is not recorded that Thomas did as asked but instead that he answered him, "My Lord and my God!" [33] Perhaps one meaning of this story is that the perspective of the circle of faith which is involved must be included as an element in any rational analysis of the person of the founder of the religion.

## Muhammad, the Messenger of Allah

The story of the career of Muhammad, the founder of Islam, is turbulent, and the interpretations of his message are controversial. This is especially true of Christian biographers, probably due in large measure to the centuries of conflict and violence between the Christian and the Muslim. As we did with the first three men in this chapter we will describe Muhammad's leadership in terms of the times in which he lived, the man himself, and the key event which, from the standpoint of history, made his leadership successful. Finally, consideration will be given to a possible interpretation of the meaning of Muhammad as the Messenger of Allah from the point of view of Muslim faith.

The inhabitants of Arabia in the sixth century A.D. tended to be animists, or, at best, polytheists, although there were many communities of Jews and Christians scattered over the area. The existence of these communities is an important

[33] John 20:24-29.

element in Muhammad's experience since from one point of view Islam is a biblical heresy, and the basic doctrines of that religion have their equivalents in Jewish and Christian teaching. It has been suggested that the religious situation of that day was not much different from that faced by Abraham, or even Moses, with the exception that there was this minority of Jewish and Christian believers.

Muhammad was born about A.D. 570 in the city of Mecca in southwest Arabia. His father, who was of the important Quraysh tribe, died before he was born and he was cared for by his mother and grandfather until he was six, and then by his uncle, Abu Talib. As a young man Muhammad traveled about the Near East with caravans of traders and learned quite a bit about the area and the various religious traditions of the Jews and Christians. At the age of twenty-five Muhammad married a wealthy widow, Khadijah, who was about fifteen years his senior. They had a happy life together, although only one of their six children, their daughter Fatima, survived to maturity.

When Muhammad was about forty he began to spend some time in meditation, until one day, in a cave near Mecca, he had a vision of the angel Gabriel who spoke to him with words that have been preserved in the Qur'an as the earliest revelation to the Prophet:

> Recite, in the name of thy Lord who has created,
> Created man from clots of blood.
> Recite, seeing that thy Lord is the most generous,
> Who has taught by the pen,
> Taught man what he did not know.[34]

This experience both frightened and troubled Muhammad, and even caused him to doubt his sanity, but Khadijah encouraged him to believe in himself, and in the message which he received in this and succeeding visions. In a series of revelations he was told that he had been chosen as a messenger

[34] Jeffery, *Islam*, Sura XCVI:1-5, p. 4.

(rasul)of the one true God, Allah, to condemn the idolatry of mankind and to call them back to the worship of Allah. Muhammad's attacks on the religious and moral practices of his fellow Meccans led to strong opposition to him and his message, but his uncle, who was very influential in the affairs of the powerful Meccan Quraysh tribe, defended and protected him. Things went hard for him, however, and became desperate when both Khadijah and Abu Talib died in the same week. Some of his followers fled to Abyssinia and established a Muslim community there. Others moved to Yathrib, a city about one hundred and fifty miles to the northeast of Mecca. They were warmly welcomed in Yathrib, and because of the importance of this city in the rise of Islam its name was later changed to Medina, a word which means "city," designating, in this case, the city par excellence. Finally, in July of 622, Muhammad himself fled to Medina to escape a plot to assassinate him and became the leader of the Muslim community there. This event is called the Hegirah, or "flight," and marks the beginning of the Muslim calendar. Soon he was ruler, judge, and religious leader, all at the same time, but the future of this new movement was most precarious. As head of the Muslim community in Medina, Muhammad soon was faced with a serious economic problem. His followers could not all resume the occupations they had practiced in Mecca, and a constant flow of refugees from the continuing persecution added daily to the demand for food and other necessities.

Then occurred two events, both military in nature, which changed everything. At this time the Prophet permitted what the non-Muslim has often labeled an action of dubious morality. Arab custom permitted caravans to travel in the month of Rajab without armed guard, since it was considered a sacred month in which such a truce was traditionally observed. But by sanction of a divine revelation Muhammad permitted his followers to raid a caravan in the sacred month and to keep much of the spoil. This meant that the Muslim community was enriched by this act, and it also had the effect of attracting many more followers to the movement by the promise of personal gain. The second event occurred in the following year when an army of one thousand Meccans attacked about three hundred of Muhammad's followers. The greatly outnumbered Muslims defeated the superior force at the Battle of Badr, offering further proof to the faithful that Allah was fighting for them. From then on, although the fortunes of the new movement had some serious setbacks, things went essentially in its favor. By the time of Muhammad's death in 632 most of the tribes of the Arabian Peninsula had sworn allegiance to Muhammad and to Allah.

The historian, then, might conclude that Islam arose through a combination of at least three factors. A young, vigorous leader, proclaiming a simple but forceful message, announced himself to be the prophet of the true God, Allah. As certification he claimed direct revelation from this God. The low level of religion and culture in Arabia meant that the times were ripe for such a clear and forceful message. The desire of his followers for power, along with his own religious fervor, gave rise to a new community. By successful military action the authority of this community prevailed. The events of the successful raid on an undefended caravan, and the miracle of the victory over strong odds at the Battle of Badr, saved the young movement from being smothered in infancy. This success continued with the result that within a century after the Prophet's death Islam had spread, by both peaceful and military means, to a wide belt of territory that formed an empire which stretched from Spain to India.

Instead of this somewhat jaundiced recounting of economic and military factors which were involved in the spread of Islam, a Muslim might view the origins of his religion from an entirely different perspective. He would, of course, be one who had become a Muslim by affirming the creed: "There is no God except Allah and Muhammad is the Messenger of Allah." His faith in Muhammad would include the conviction that the Prophet of Allah was the final messenger from God and that the mighty Qur'an was Allah's final message to man-
138

kind to show the way to true salvation. Thus in Surah XXXIII:36 we read: "It is not for any believing man or believing woman, when Allah and His messenger have decided an affair, to have any choice in their affair, and whosoever opposes Allah and His messenger has manifestly strayed into error." [35] In other words, to a Muslim the event which marks the beginning of Islam is the merciful act of Allah in choosing Muhammad to be his messenger and the one through whom he gave his gift of the mighty Qur'an. This is the beginning and the end of Muslim faith, and without this conviction no one can be a Muslim. In fact, it is not too much of an oversimplification to state that the essential beliefs which separate the Jew, Christian, and Muslim are that the Jew claims Moses as the true spokesman for the God of Abraham, the Christian claims that the final revelation, which superseded the Law of Moses, came through Jesus Christ, and the Muslim hails Muhammad as the Seal of the prophets, the one through whom the final revelation, the Qur'an, was given.

Muslim piety builds on this faith, and there are many myths and legends surrounding the life of Muhammad giving testimony to their devotion. His birth was foreordained and attended with marvelous signs; before the Hegirah he was transported in a "night journey" to Jerusalem and to heaven itself;[36] and his character, so often assailed by non-Muslims, was without fault. The fact that Muhammad took ten wives after the death of his beloved Khedijah, for instance, is shown to be in response to Allah's commands, sometimes only reluctantly obeyed by Muhammad.[37] These marriages were usually entered into to ensure security and income for the widows of comrades-in-arms and were always contracted without lustful intent.[38] The famous raid on the unarmed caravan was actually not a raid, but instead the Meccans had set a trap to entice the Muslims out into the open that they might

[35] *Ibid.,* p. 13.
[36] Dr. G. I. Kheirallah, *Islam and the Arabian Prophet* (New York: Islamic Publishing Company, 1938) "Al-Israa," pp. 47 ff.
[37] *Ibid.,* pp. 110-11.
[38] *Ibid.*

destroy them.[39] Only Allah's divine intervention saved them from disaster. We find Alfred Guillaume stating that "Islam goes far beyond the Jewish and Christian veneration for prophets as men inspired by God to reveal his will to the world, in claiming that the prophets, and especially the seal of the prophets, were without sin and infallible." [40]

## O Master, Let Me Walk with Thee!

With these brief sketches of the four founders before us we conclude this chapter by asking the question: "What does it mean to follow a master?" It would appear that it means something quite different for the followers of different leaders. If one is a follower of the Buddha his vocation as a disciple means that he must accept Gautama as the Enlightened One, and to follow him in treading the Noble Eightfold Path requires a denial of all attachments to the world, and ultimately, denial of one's very self. But this denial of oneself is not found in service to the Buddha, or to a god, or to one's fellow man, but rather is intended to lead to the extinction of self, to nirvana. To facilitate this striving one joins the Sangha, the "order" of monks, those who also have severed all ties with kinsmen and loved ones. One follows the Buddha in order to save oneself, and in the earliest tradition there is no god who can help. One must follow the strenuous path of self-salvation which leads to the cessation of all desires.

The way of Master K'ung requires that Confucius be followed as the one who truly understood the way to personal and social happiness and well-being. And this way is the way of the ancient, feudal Chinese society of China's mythical golden past, a time when everyone knew his proper place in society, the youths were obedient to their elders, and the elders and superiors were just and kind to their inferiors. Though there is no god to help, it is believed that Confucius followed

---

[39] Mohammed Marmaduke Pickthall, The Meaning of the Glorious Koran: an Explanatory Translation (New York: The New American Library, 1954), pp. xvii-xviii.

[40] Islam (Baltimore: Penguin Books, 1954), p. 118.

perfectly the way of t'ien, so that all that is necessary to bring about peace, prosperity, and happiness for the entire world of man and nature is for all to follow Master K'ung and his way.

To follow Jesus as Lord and Master means that one must begin with the conviction that God really did reveal himself in the life, death, and resurrection of Jesus. One must join the ranks of such believers and become a member of the church, the fellowship of those called from death to life by their faith. One must accept the meaning of the biblical drama as a true interpretation of existence with its creator God who is Lord of life and Judge of all men, for it is only in this circle of faith that the Lordship of Christ makes consistent sense.

The follower of the prophet Muhammad joins the Muslim brotherhood when he recites the creed: "There is no God but Allah and Muhammad is the Prophet of Allah." He thereby submits to Allah's will as revealed in the Glorious Qur'an and is committed to the cause of bringing all the world under the rule of Allah.

It would appear, then, that it is not the same thing to follow each of these men, and one cannot follow all four, since each religion makes claims upon the loyalties of men which are mutually exclusive. Yet most men need to have a leader to follow, one who offers direction, meaning, and stability to one's life. This was cruelly demonstrated in Hitler's "post-Christian" Germany, or Mussolini's fascist Italy, and was the basis of the cult of personality in Russia or of any totalitarian state. In the biblical context, which stresses the necessity of choice, Jesus said that no one can serve two masters. In the context of the varied claims of the world's religions it can be affirmed that no one can serve more than one of these four masters since each must be served within the context of his own circle of faith.

CHAPTER 6

# WATCHMAN, TELL US OF THE NIGHT!

Chapter three placed emphasis upon salvation in this present life as a concern common to all religions. Man seeks the help of supernatural forces to find meaning and security in this life. He desires to be delivered from sickness to health, from famine to plenty, and from despair to hope. Although this present life is a major concern of all religions, from the very beginning of history we find that man also has a concern to affirm some kind of purpose beyond the grave, to be assured of some form of survival after death. The earliest human remains from which the archaeologist reconstructs possible social practices of prehistoric man almost always involve burial of the dead. It is assumed that this practice was performed with some idea of survival in mind. The great pyramids of ancient Egypt testify to the desire on the part of the nobility of man's earliest civilization to perpetuate existence. Each of the great living religions, as well, has a teaching about human destiny as part of its message of salvation.

There are those who attempt to trace the beginnings of all

religion to some kind of cult of the dead. This is undoubtedly an oversimplification which places too much importance on man's fear of death, but there is no denying the fact that a great deal has been written on the subject. This is probably due, at least in part, to the simple fact that death must remain the ultimate mystery for man, since no human being has experienced death. There are, of course, perennial attempts on the part of the living to communicate with the departed, and religious history is replete with tales of necromancers. In our day we have the continuing efforts of the various spiritualist groups to "break the death barrier," as it were, or the attempts of students of E.S.P. to develop a scientific methodology to demonstrate and to facilitate their attempts at communication by means of extrasensory perception, not only between living persons, but also between the living and the dead. Even though any claim to knowledge about the existence of the nature of life after death is not verifiable, and quite often a good deal of fun is poked at those who are seriously concerned with this problem, the vast majority of persons of the world's teeming population subscribe to some sort of belief in life after death, and interest and speculation on the subject are intense.

The fact that the various religious traditions have preserved many writings by their skeptics and apostles of despair who have denied that there is any real meaning to existence, or any possible hope of survival after death, is negative testimony to the importance of this problem. Koheleth said long ago: "For of the wise man as of the fool there is no enduring remembrance, seeing that in the days to come all will have been long forgotten. How the wise man dies just like the fool! So I hated life, because what is done under the sun was grievous to me; for all is vanity and a striving after wind." [1] The harsh honesty of Job who refused to be placated by the orthodox dogmas of his friends obviously was an attack on the piety of the author's day:

[1] Eccl. 2:16-17.

> Will any teach God knowledge,
> seeing that he judges those that are on high?
> One dies in full prosperity,
> being wholly at ease and secure,
> his body full of fat
> and the marrow of his bones moist.
> Another dies in bitterness of soul,
> never having tasted of good.
> They lie down alike in the dust,
> and the worms cover them.[2]

The apostle Paul is quite realistic when he admits the possibility that the Christian claim to immortality might be groundless. He states:

If there is no resurrection of the dead, then Christ has not been raised; if Christ has not been raised, then our preaching is in vain and your faith is in vain. We are even found to be misrepresenting God, because we testified of God that he raised Christ, whom he did not raise if it is true that the dead are not raised. For if the dead are not raised, then Christ has not been raised. If Christ has not been raised, your faith is futile and you are still in your sins. Then those also who have fallen asleep in Christ have perished. If for this life only we have hoped in Christ, we are of all men most to be pitied.[3]

My point in quoting from Ecclesiastes, Job, and Paul is to stress that in these passages from the Bible, and similar passages from other religious traditions as well, we are not dealing with second-rate minds, nor with sheer superstition, but instead with honest, thoughtful and realistic attempts to understand reality. There is a willingness to admit that the answer of faith is not the only possible one. In fact, in the various religions what is often in later years taken for arbitrariness and dogma had its origins in lively debate between schools of thought and between men of faith and the outsider. Of course, when Paul, for instance, goes on to affirm what is for

[2] Job 21:22-26.
[3] I Cor. 15:13-19.

144

him the fact of Christ's resurrection, he is using the language of faith. "Lo! I tell you a mystery. We shall not all sleep, but we shall all be changed, in a moment, in the twinkling of an eye, at the last trumpet." [4] It is unfortunate that much of the quarrel between science and religion in this area of belief has failed to take into account the differences between religious concepts and the spatial and temporal considerations of science. A common canard aimed at medieval Christian theologians is that they spent a great deal of time arguing about how many angels could dance on the point of a needle. Usually when this remark is made the critic fails to go on and point out that the real purpose of such argument had to do with whether or not an angel occupied space, since it was part of the debate of the scholastics on form and reality. Instead the remark is intended to make theologians, and perhaps Christianity, appear silly.

At the same time the record of the church in this conflict between science and faith is not enviable. Copernicus, who displaced the Ptolemaic earth-centered cosmos with the notion of the solar system and orbiting planets, as well as Galileo, Newton, and Darwin, were attacked viciously by church leaders as heretics, or even as minions of the devil himself. The Scopes "monkey trial" of 1925 in Dayton, Tennessee, is still recent enough to be a vivid reminder of the threat to orthodoxy made by scientific contributions to our understanding of the nature, size, and age of the universe. The church has been forced, again and again, to retract or restate its criticism and opposition to such scientific discoveries, and this continues to be a most sensitive area in academic and ecclesiastical circles.

At the turn of the century the nature of the scientific opposition to a belief in life after death was forcefully and clearly stated by Bertrand Russell in his oft-quoted essay, "A Free Man's Worship." He wrote:

That man is the product of causes which had no prevision of the end they were achieving; that his origin, his growth, his hopes and

[4] I Cor. 15:51-52.

fears, his loves and his beliefs, are but the outcome of accidental collocations of atoms; that no fire, no heroism, no intensity of thought and feeling, can preserve an individual life beyond the grave; that all the labors of the ages, all the devotion, all the inspiration, all the noonday brightness of human genius, are destined to extinction in the vast death of the solar system, and that the whole temple of man's achievement must inevitably be buried beneath the debris of a universe in ruins—all these things, if not quite beyond dispute, are yet so nearly certain that no philosophy which rejects them can hope to stand.[5]

Coming from one with such powerful intellect, and in light of the great contributions that Lord Russell has made to modern science and mathematics, such words cannot go unheeded by any religious person. In fact, the attempts on the part of some Christians to respond to this sort of challenge are what have led to such recent debates in theological circles as the suggestion that we "demythologize the Bible," [6] and the "honest to God" [7] controversy. It sometimes would appear, however, that the defenders of Christianity, both conservative and liberal, are too eager to answer science on its own ground rather than to try to interpret religion in terms of its own language. Thus if one takes Russell literally it is to be wondered how it is that he can, later in his essay, use such terms as "truth," "beauty," and "perfection" if he is himself but "the outcome of accidental collocations of atoms." That is to say, if he has no better explanation for a Beethoven symphony or the Brahms Requiem, how can he be so sure what the end of existence is? The New Testament book of the Revelation to John, like Russell, foretells a cataclysmic doom, and insofar as each author is using the language of myth and symbol there appears to be no good reason to prefer the scientist to the man of faith.

[5] Fifth paragraph (in part).
[6] Cf., e.g., Hans Werner Bartsch, ed., Kerygma and Myth: a Theological Debate. Tr. by Reginald H. Fuller (2nd ed.; Naperville, Ill.: Alec R. Allenson, 1962, 1964).
[7] John A. T. Robinson, Honest to God (Philadelphia: The Westminster Press, 1963).

### Myth as the Symbolic Language of Faith

To suggest that Russell and the New Testament are both using the language of myth gets us into the heart of the problem of thinking about life after death. The language of science and the language of faith have this much in common: Each often must resort to symbolic language because the subject under discussion cannot be conceptualized or grasped by the use of ordinary terms, either because it deals with things that are so infinitesimal or so vast that they really escape clear comprehension, or because they deal with subjects that are not reducible to time-space language. Recently I watched a National Educational Television astronomy program on the subject of "Stars." Some of the subject matter was fairly comprehensible, but for some the imagination boggled. For instance, in using an illustration to explain the extreme density of matter in a "dwarf star," the narrator remarked that he had been told that if all the matter in the Empire State Building were to be isolated from the energy, and the bits of matter were to be placed in a dish, the total amount of matter would occupy a space smaller than that of the head of a pin! Again, when astrophysicists are attempting to calculate the size of the universe they use the term "light-year," which is about 5.87 trillion miles—the distance light can travel in one year (traveling day and night) at 186 thousand miles a second. The term "light-year" is a useful symbol, but it is also incomprehensible. Some astronomers are now suggesting that the known universe might be some 14 billion light-years across—they don't know—and they have no way of telling whether or not there is a limit or boundary to the universe. One theory even posits an antiuniverse, a universe just like ours in every respect, except that everything in it is exactly the opposite of ours. But this theory does not help us understand what might be beyond this antiuniverse, or in which direction from us it might be. The mystery of the atom and the mystery of the macrocosm can be explored and described but never explained, and it is necessary to use symbolic language merely to describe them.

In the Gospel of Mark when Jesus was arrested and brought before a council of priests, "the high priest stood up in the midst, and asked Jesus, 'Have you no answer to make? What is it that these men testify against you?' But he was silent and made no answer. Again the high priest asked him, 'Are you the Christ, the Son of the Blessed?' And Jesus said, 'I am; and you will see the Son of man sitting at the right hand of Power, and coming with the clouds of heaven.'" [8] For this Jesus was accused of blasphemy and condemned to death.

Now if one were to take this reference to the Son of man coming on the clouds of heaven out of the context of the mythology of Jesus' day, and were to set it in the context of the Copernican revolution and our contemporary astronauts, one would have to reject out of hand the biblical notion of a three-level universe with heaven above, the earth around us, and hell beneath, and along with it Jesus' word on the coming Son of man. But the Bible itself appears to warn us against taking such language too literally. There has been a long and acrimonious controversy, for instance, over the Genesis stories of creation, with participants attempting to defend or refute the literal meaning of the stories. Yet the author of the book of Job has Yahweh ask Job:

> Where were you when I laid the foundation of the
>    earth?
> Tell me, if you have understanding.
> Who determined its measurements—surely you
>    know!
> Or who stretched the line upon it?
> On what were its bases sunk,
>    or who laid its cornerstone,
> when the morning stars sang together,
>    and all the sons of God shouted for joy? [9]

[8] Mark 14:60-62.
[9] 38:4-7.

148

This theophany appears to suggest that man does not have all the answers, and that perhaps he does not need to know everything. In this connection it is interesting to note how frequently the great religious teachers had a lack of concern for details about the beginnings and ends of the universe but, on the contrary, had a concern that was quite existential for present meaning and decision. Thus we read in the Analects of Confucius that "Tzu-lu asked how one should serve ghosts and spirits. The Master said, Till you have learnt to serve men, how can you serve ghosts? Tzu-lu then ventured upon a question about the dead. The Master said, Till you know about the living, how are you to know about the dead?" [10] Waley comments that "all that is meant by the reply . . . is that for the Chün-tzu [Confucian gentleman] questions about the existence led by the dead are of secondary importance as compared to those connected with the handling of living men." [11]

In the case of Gautama, one early Buddhist scripture emphasizes that he tried to discourage his disciples from being anxious about the problem of whether, when one dies and attains nirvana, he then exists in some kind of life after death, and if so, what the nature of it might be.

And what, Mālunkyā-putta, have I not explained? Whether the world is eternal I have not explained, whether the world is not eternal . . . whether a Tathāgata is both nonexistent and not nonexistent after death I have not explained. And why, Mālunkyā-putta, have I not explained this? Because this, Mālunkyā-putta, is not useful, it is not concerned with the principle of a religious life, does not conduce to aversion, absence of passion, cessation, tranquility, supernatural faculty, perfect knowledge, Nirvāna, and therefore I have not explained it.[12]

Gautama's meaning would appear to be, at least in part, that the state of being in nirvana, or at least the achievement

[10] Waley, Analects, XI:11.
[11] Ibid., p. 32.
[12] Majjhima Nikāya, Sutta 63, tr. by E. J. Thomas, Buddhist Scriptures, quoted by Hamilton, Buddhism, p. 56.

149

of nirvana, was not to be compared with any earthly experience. Whatever it is, it is not something which can be described in ordinary terms. It can be partially experienced in this present life and the man of Buddhist faith can accept it as a positive good, but the nature of nirvana is such that one is not able to reduce it to logical and concrete terms.

When Jesus was pushed to commit himself on the question of the resurrection of the dead, he approached the question as one which cannot be answered on the basis of human logic but indicated instead that it lay in the area of faith.

And Sadducees came to him, who say that there is no resurrection; and they asked him a question, saying, "Teacher, Moses wrote for us that if a man's brother dies and leaves a wife, but leaves no child, the man must take the wife, and raise up children for his brother. There were seven brothers; the first took a wife, and when he died left no children; and the second took her, and died, leaving no children; and the third likewise; and the seven left no children. Last of all the woman also died. In the resurrection whose wife will she be? For the seven had her as wife."

Jesus said to them, "Is not this why you are wrong, that you know neither the scriptures nor the power of God? For when they rise from the dead, they neither marry nor are given in marriage, but are like angels in heaven. And as for the dead being raised, have you not read in the book of Moses, in the passage about the bush, how God said to him, 'I am the God of Abraham, and the God of Isaac, and the God of Jacob'? He is not God of the dead, but of the living; you are quite wrong." [13]

The Gospel of Mark informs us that Jesus proclaimed that "The time is fulfilled, and the kingdom of God is at hand; repent, and believe in the gospel." [14] It would appear, however, that Jesus refused to commit himself as to just when God would inaugurate his kingdom. Or rather, there is no agreement among Christians on what he did mean, as witness the many interpretations given to the nature of the eschaton

[13] Mark 12:18-27.
[14] 1:14.

(time of the end) throughout Christian history. In the thirteenth chapter of Mark we find almost in juxtaposition the following teachings: "Truly I say to you, this generation will not pass away before all these things take place. . . . But of that day or that hour no one knows, not even the angels in heaven, nor the Son, but only the Father." [15] Ever since Jesus' day men have tried to figure out when the end of the age will come, apparently ignoring another word of Jesus: "An evil and adulterous generation seeks for a sign." [16]

It is interesting that for each of these three, Confucius, Gautama, and Jesus, there is wide variation of interpretation by his followers concerning his views about life after death. Yet it is very likely that this disagreement stems in each case from two basic errors. The first error is to assume that the words of such a teacher about life after death can be taken in a literal sense. In spite of the warnings of these men their followers attempt to puzzle out logical answers to questions which are framed in such a manner that they simply do not fit the problems involved. Although Jesus, for instance, is reported to have rebuked the Sadducees for their lack of faith—"Is not this why you are wrong, that you know neither the scriptures nor the power of God?"—his followers still make the same error by seeking to wring concrete answers to their own lack of faith out of Jesus' words. His teachings in this case deal with an area outside normal human experience and can be properly understood only when viewed as employing the symbolic and mythological language of faith.

The second error which compounds the felony of seeking to reduce the language of faith to the language of everyday logic stems from this very desire to make one's faith "walk on all fours," as it were. It is not enough for the average follower simply to trust, to have faith in, the words of the teacher. The teachings must be given concrete content and made to yield a positive statement. What results from this forcing of the words, however, is not to capture the sure faith of Jesus or

[15] Vss. 30, 32.
[16] Matt. 16:4.

151

Gautama. We find instead that it leads to a prosaic undergirding of the lack of faith of the so-called believer. From such false approaches all too often come arbitrary creedal statements and dogmatic conclusions which replace the vigor and mystery of faith.

We have been using the words "myth" and "mythology" throughout this book without attempting to define or defend our use of these terms. The language of myth has come under intensive study in recent decades with real benefit to students of religion. To many people the word "myth" connotes a story that is not true, perhaps because the church fathers labeled the Greek and Roman myths as untrue because, according to their faith, they were about false gods. Actually a myth is a story whose subject matter concerns a god or gods. Since a myth is a story about divine activity, every religion must use the language of myth to describe supernatural events. Instead of being concerned with whether a myth is true or false, therefore, one should seek to understand what a myth means to a man of faith. Since actions of the supernatural cannot be reduced to everyday language without distortion, it follows that the language of myth must be symbolic and poetic in form. The biblical myths in Genesis 1–3, for instance, employ poetic and symbolic language to tell of God's actions in creating the world. In the book of Revelation we find a myth telling of God's purpose for the future, where the faith of John of Patmos is given expression in symbolic and poetic language. Since such stories are not to be interpreted literally—any more than one of Aesop's fables is to be taken literally—but at the same time they do convey the faith of a religion, Reinhold Niebuhr has referred to myths as "deceivers, yet true." [17] If they are interpreted literally they lead to misunderstanding, yet they contain profound religious truths which are apparent to the man of faith.

What can we say, then, about the nature of "things to come," about the myths of human destiny in the various re-

[17] *Beyond Tragedy: Essays on the Christian Interpretation of History* (New York: Charles Scribner's Sons, 1937), chap. 1.

ligions? The first thing to notice is that there are many common elements in the mythologies of mankind. There are, for instance, widespread stories of the creation of the first man and woman, of a "garden of Eden," stories about a great flood which almost destroyed the human race, and many other cosmogonic myths which are common stock in many religions. There also are many similar or parallel myths about the future, about life after death. Thus most religions have myths about a heaven for the good, and a hell for the bad. Many concern a savior who is to come in the future to redeem mankind —the Buddha Maitreya, the Muslim Mahdi, the return to earth of the Hindu god, Vishnu, in some animal or human form, to mention only three besides the Jewish Messiah and the Second Coming of Christ. Such common denominators in the "mythology of all races" are, to many persons, just one more proof that all religions are basically the same. I would prefer to trace these similar myths to the common racial experience of mankind in the countless millennia before the great religions arose, and also to the simple fact that the limitations of human language, about which we have been talking, mean that man's religious hopes and aspirations can be expressed in only a limited number of ways.

If we focus our attention on a few teachings about the future which appear to be distinctive and different, rather than on those which are similar in nature, we should find further documentation for our thesis of "circles of faith." We should also be able to show how these distinctive teachings are in harmony with other tenets of the circle of faith in which they occur. At the same time we should become more aware of why a religious belief or practice which might seem strange, or even repulsive, to an outsider might be taken for granted as something quite natural and normal by a member of that faith. For our purposes we have chosen a basic teaching about the future from each of the three major circles of faith. For the circle of faith of the Indian religions we have chosen the belief in rebirth which is common to Hinduism, Jainism, Buddhism, and the Sikhs; for the biblical, monotheistic religions we have chosen the doctrine of bodily resurrection; for East Asia, the great concern for the past and the way of the ancestors.

## The Indian Doctrine of Rebirth

Throughout this book we have linked the belief in rebirth, that is, in a cycle of births and deaths for each living being, with the religions that arose in India. This does not mean that the idea of rebirth is foreign to the thinking of those in the biblical or East Asian circles of faith. This was made quite clear a few years ago when there was a flurry of interest in rebirth in the United States during the controversy over "the search for Bridie Murphy." One of the main roots of Western culture is that of the Platonic tradition, and in Plato's dialogue, *The Republic*, at the end of the apocalyptic myth in the tenth book, there is a passage explaining the differences in human nature in terms of rebirth and the forgetfulness brought about by drinking from the "river of Unmindfulness" between births. Part of the meaning of Socrates' dictum, "know thyself," is that the truth about a subject is to be found within you, since you learned it in previous lives. Unfortunately most persons drink too deeply from this Lethean spring between births, and knowledge is repressed. With this conviction Socrates employed a method of education which used questions to awaken and bring out of the student this knowledge which lay dormant in his memory. In spite of such connections with this world view, the doctrine of rebirth is not normative in the Western tradition, any more than it appears to be native to the thought of East Asia. Much of the Buddhism of Japan, for instance, does not concern itself with rebirth as a basic issue, even though this would appear to have been central to Gautama's message.

If you but scratch the surface of Indian thought, however, the concern with metempsychosis, the rebirth of the soul in physical form, is immediately evident. To Westerners the description of a Jain holy man carefully sweeping the path in front of him with a soft brush, so as to move gently out of

154

harm's way any insect life, is familiar. One of the earliest, and very influential, accounts of everyday life in India, that by Abbé Dubois, has helped to familiarize us with this concern for all living beings. He said of the Jains:

Their fear of destroying life is carried to such a length that the women, before smearing the floor with cow-dung, are in the habit of sweeping it very gently first, so as to remove, without hurting them, any insects that may be there. If they neglected this precaution they would run the risk of crushing one of these little creatures whilst rubbing the floor, which would be the source of the keenest regret to them.[18]

Far from being merely popular superstition, however, or merely an exotic custom, this practice does reflect an ingrained view of the nature of man in all Indian thought. No matter where you turn it is easy to illustrate this concern. In the Bhagavad-Gita, for instance, which is the most important scripture to millions of Hindus, such a reference occurs just after the long passage we quoted earlier, in chapter four, in connection with nonviolence in Hinduism.

> Nay, but as when one layeth
> His worn-out robes away,
> And, taking new ones, sayeth,
> "These will I wear today!"
> So putteth by the spirit
> Lightly its garb of flesh,
> And passeth to inherit
> A resident afresh.[19]

The Laws of Manu, which serve as the basis for life and thought for most Hindus, make constant reference to transmigration. In Chapter VI of these Laws, which discusses the kind of thought proper for the ascetic, we read:

[18] Hindu Manners, Customs and Ceremonies. Tr. by Henry K. Beauchamp (3rd ed.; New York: Oxford University Press, 1905), p. 698.
[19] Arnold, chap. 2.

Let him reflect on the transmigration of men, caused by their sinful deeds, on their falling into hell, and on the torments in the world of Yama. On the separation from their dear ones, on their union with hated men, on their being overpowered by age and being tormented with diseases, on the departure of the individual soul from this body and its new birth in (another) womb, and on its wanderings through ten thousand millions of existences, on the infliction of pain on embodied (spirits), which is caused by demerit, and the gain of eternal bliss, which is caused by the attainment of their highest aim (gained through) spiritual merit.[20]

We have already referred to the Jataka tales, the stories about the many lives of the Buddha in various animal forms before his final reincarnation and enlightenment, as well as to the way in which both Jainism and Buddhism were a protest against the spiritual monopoly claimed by the Brahmans as their reward for accumulated virtue from previous existences. In addition, the religion of the Sikhs, founded by Nanak (A.D. 1469-1538), although it was a reform movement within Hinduism under Muslim influence, also accepts the Hindu doctrines of karma and transmigration of souls. In other words, this important teaching of rebirth is firmly entrenched in Indian religious thought and is assumed, without critical examination, to be normative by most Indians. The question, therefore, that is important for us to ask is what it means in the context of the Indian circle of faith.

At least three important corollaries to rebirth as an aspect of belief can be shown. The first is the way in which transmigration serves to describe the Hindu view of the nature of man and to help account for human and social differences. The class structure of Hinduism, which undoubtedly arose in Vedic times out of the Aryan conquest of India, is given religious approval by this doctrine. One Hindu term for the four social classes is *jati*, meaning "birth." A person is born into a class, but in Indian thought this birth is not predicated on the social

---

[20] Sections 61-64. G. Bühler, tr., Sacred Books of the East, XXV (London: Oxford University Press, 1886), 209-10.

status of the parents. Instead, the rebirth of a soul into low or high class parentage is the result of the accumulated good or bad karma from previous lives of the soul that has been reborn.

A second corollary is that rebirth supplies an answer to the problem of human suffering and misery. The Laws of Manu state that "by his origin alone a [Brahman] is a deity even for the gods." [21] If one is of fortunate, Brahman birth, this is his reward for all his past good karma. If he is born of low class, or crippled, blind, or otherwise defective, such misfortunes are deserved punishment for past deeds. I was in the cafeteria line at my university with a Hindu student one day when I asked him how he felt about rebirth. He replied that if someone were to bump into him and spill his tray of food he would feel that it was because he had done the same to someone in a previous birth. O'Malley sums up the view in popular Hinduism in this way:

As he sows, so shall he reap, or, to quote a Hindu saying, "the body is the field, the soul is the cultivator; virtue and vice are seeds, and the soul must reap as it sows." This is an inexorable law, the working of cause and effect. If there is a balance of good to a man's credit, he gets the benefit of it by being reborn on a higher plane. If he has given himself up to wickedness, he sinks lower at rebirth. Each man lays up a stock of good and bad deeds and, so to speak, accumulates moral capital. The debit of vice can be wiped out by the credit of virtue, and men may thus rise on stepping stones of their dead selves to higher things.[22]

This leads to the third corollary, which is that rebirth serves as a powerful sanction for ethical living. This is to be understood, of course, in the context of the Hindu social structure which it helps to support. Chapter XII of the *Laws of Manu* is on "Transmigration," and begins with the statement: "Action, which springs from the mind, from speech, and from

[21] *Ibid.*, XI:85, p. 447.
[22] L. S. S. O'Malley, *Popular Hinduism: The Religion of the Masses* (New York: The Macmillan Company, 1935), p. 8.

157

the body, produces either good or evil results; by action are caused the (various) conditions of men, the highest, the middling, and the lowest." [23] Of course it makes an unbalanced impression to quote only the teachings of priestly, Brahman scriptures which stress the following of one's dharma (duty) as the only way to raise oneself, through many rebirths, until final release is obtained. Not only did Jainism and Buddhism revolt against this priestly monopoly, but in Hinduism the way of salvation by devotion, bhakti-marga, also became available to those of lower birth. Here the hope for a better rebirth, or even a possible temporary (in cosmic terms) life with the Lord Vishnu, is offered as a sanction for righteous living. After the tremendous theophany in chapter XI of the Gita, Vishnu, through his avatar Krishna, tells how one, by high ethical living, might come near to the deity. Chapter XII ends with this statement:

> But most of all I love
> Those happy ones to whom 'tis life to live
> In single fervid faith and love unseeing,
> Eating the blessed Amrit of my Being! [24]

Even though one must face future rebirths after spending a blessed aeon with Vishnu, that "temporary" life with the God of many millions of years' duration according to earth's time exerts a strong appeal to the faithful to live a life of virtue. It would appear, in other words, that metempsychosis is not necessarily an enervating doctrine but instead serves quite often as a dynamic to high ethical living.

### The Biblical Doctrine of the Resurrection of the Body

Just as the idea of rebirth in its literal form is puzzling to most Jews and Christians, the idea of the physical resurrection of the body is abhorrent to many in Asia, and even poses a

[23] P. 483.
[24] Arnold, Bhagavad-Gītā.

problem to some Christians who repeat the phrase in the Apostles' Creed, "I believe in the resurrection of the body," as part of their regular worship. With such fare as the story of Frankenstein, the Tales of Edgar Allan Poe, and Charles Addams' cartoons to strengthen one's negative reactions to the notion of reanimated corpses rising from graves and tombs, it is possible to understand why this biblical doctrine might be offensive to one of another circle of faith. To the Hindu or Buddhist the body is a corrupt, basically evil thing which entombs the soul. This is not much different from the Greek saying, soma sema, a pun which means that the body is the tomb of the spirit. In fact, the Apostles' Creed itself represents a compromise at this point for it adds, after the phrase about bodily resurrection, the words "and the life everlasting."

But it is not only the Apostles' Creed which attempts to soften the harsh meaning of a literal physical resurrection. The New Testament, especially, allegorizes and spiritualizes the teaching even while insisting that it be retained. Earlier in this chapter we referred to the story of the Sadducees questioning Jesus in a literal manner about the resurrection. Jesus affirmed his belief in the resurrection but also said that when persons rise from the dead they are like the angels in heaven. The Gospel of John also emphasizes the difference between the physical and spiritual resurrection in the story of Lazarus. "Then Jesus . . . came to the tomb; it was a cave, and a stone lay upon it. Jesus said, 'Take away the stone.' Martha, the sister of the dead man, said to him, 'Lord, by this time there will be an odor, for he has been dead four days.' Jesus said to her, 'Did I not tell you that if you would believe you would see the glory of God?' " [25]

The Talmudic teachers discussed the question of the nature of the resurrection in the Messianic age for one who had died in a distant land, or even for a sailor who had gone down with his ship. Such a one would find a tunnel created for him to roll through until he arose in his own village.[26] In our day a

[25] John 11:38-40.
[26] Moore, Judaism, II, 379-80.

Jew or Christian interpreting the doctrine literally might be greatly distressed to learn that his son had gone down in flames over the Pacific Ocean. Was his body badly burned? Was it blown to bits? Without proper burial how can he rise from the dead at the end of the age? Such questions are not uncommon, and while they may be mistaken and show misunderstanding of the meaning of the myth, they also show the need for explanation and interpretation, even to the man of faith. The apostle Paul faced this sort of problem in his discussion of the resurrection of the dead which he directed to the Corinthian churches. Following the method of question and answer used by teachers of that day he wrote:

> But some one will ask, "How are the dead raised? With what kind of body do they come?" You foolish man! What you sow does not come to life unless it dies. And what you sow is not the body which is to be, but a bare kernel, perhaps of wheat or of some other grain. But God gives it a body as he has chosen, and to each kind of seed its own body.[27]

Nevertheless, in our day the typical Christian funeral is a mixed-up affair with a great deal of money spent on embalming and burying the body, yet with a service, usually held before the burial, which assumes that the soul of the departed already is in heaven. It is not possible for us adequately to deal with this and similar problems here, but with the preceding discussion in mind let us ask what the resurrection of the dead means in the wide context of the circle of faith of biblical religions. After a brief summary of the way in which the doctrine developed we will indicate our understanding of its meaning and importance.[28]

The religions included under our designation "biblical religions" are all monotheistic, with the doctrine of a creator

[27] I Cor. 15:35-38.
[28] This is not to imply that this doctrine can be explained by evolutionary theory; at the same time there is no denying that it had a clear development. Cf. R. H. Charles, *A Critical History of a Doctrine of a Future Life* (London: Adam and Charles Black, 1899).

160

god as a common denominator. Since in this context each person is a unique creation, with a single life to live on earth, the doctrine of the resurrection of the body should be in harmony with this view of the nature of man. As was pointed out in chapter three, in these religions man's present salvation and happiness are to be achieved by obedience to the will of his creator. In early Hebrew history this was viewed in a fairly straightforward manner. In the book of Judges, for instance, the Deuteronomistic historians interpreted Hebrew history in terms of a fairly simple equation which ascribed success in war to the fact of obedience to the will of Yahweh and linked disaster with disobedience to Yahweh. Long after the time of the judges one of the psalms says:

> I have been young, and now am old;
> yet I have not seen the righteous forsaken
> or his children begging bread.[29]

Unfortunately the hard facts of experience appeared to go against this faith, and the book of Job, for instance, is a protest against the view that in this life the good are always rewarded and the wicked punished. Job raised the question of theodicy, the question of how a creator God can allow evil to dominate his creation.

One answer to this question was to advocate the belief that, although in this life things do not always go the way of the righteous, after death God has a purpose for those who are faithful to him. Early Hebraic notions about life after death reflect the view common to the ancient Near East of a cheerless survival by some in an underground abode called Sheol.[30] Here the dead existed as shades, and it appears that at first it was thought that the good and wicked were mixed together. Later there are references to Sheol as a place divided to provide a place for each group. Finally arose the belief in a spatial

[29] Ps. 37:25.
[30] Cf. Charles, A Critical History.

division, with heaven as the abode of the righteous and an underground hell for the punishment of the wicked.

Although the doctrine of a future life in hell or heaven meant that God could punish or reward after death those who obviously had not received their just deserts while alive, there was still another important consideration in this development. A doctrine parallel to belief in a future heaven and hell was that God would someday redeem the fortunes of his people and inaugurate his kingdom on earth. In this Messianic age all the righteous would be rewarded with marvelous blessings, which would surpass anything previously known to man. One of the materialistic teachings about this age of gold was that one might live a thousand years and enjoy great physical prosperity and happiness. But this hope left out of account those worthy ones who had lived in previous times, and in the late Old Testament period the doctrine of the resurrection of the dead began to appear as an answer to this problem. The book of Daniel is the classical reference for this teaching. This writing was composed about 165 B.C. to encourage the Jews in the Maccabean struggle for religious freedom and political independence against the tyranny of their Syrian rulers. As part of the encouragement to resist, even if it meant death, the author offered an apocalyptic vision of the future, concluding with these words:

At that time shall arise Michael, the great prince who has charge of your people. And there shall be a time of trouble, such as never has been since there was a nation till that time; but at that time your people shall be delivered, every one whose name shall be found written in the book. And many of those who sleep in the dust of the earth shall awake, some to everlasting life, and some to shame and everlasting contempt.[31]

This meant that the very good and the very bad of those who had lived in former times would participate in the coming reign of God. Before long this partial resurrection was ex-

[31] Dan. 12:1-2.

162

panded to include all mankind in a great resurrection at the last day. The New Testament book of Revelation describes this final judgment.

"Then I saw thrones, and seated on them were those to whom judgment was committed. Also I saw the souls of those who had been beheaded for their testimony to Jesus and for the word of God, and who had not worshiped the beast or its image. . . . They came to life again, and reigned with Christ a thousand years. The rest of the dead did not come to life again until the thousand years were ended. . . . And when the thousand years are ended, Satan will be loosed from his prison. . . . And I saw the dead, and great and small, standing before the throne. . . . And the dead were judged by what was written in the books, by what they had done. . . . [Then] Death and Hades gave up the dead in them, and all were judged by what they had done." [32]

This apocalyptic vision of God's final judgment was later to be echoed in one of the five doctrines of Islam, the Doctrine of Allah's Last Day. Two brief quotations from the Qur'an indicate something of the concrete imagery employed:

When the heavens shall be rent asunder,
And when the stars shall be dispersed,
And when the seas shall be commingled,
And when the graves shall be upturned,
A soul will know what it has sent forward and kept
    back.[33]

And again:

And those who have precedence, those who have pre-
    cedence,
They are those who are brought near
In gardens of delight,
Quite a number from the former generations,
And a few from the latter,

[32] Rev. 20:4-13 (in part).
[33] Jeffery, *Islam*, Sura LXXXII: 1-5, pp. 138-39.

163

On couches inlaid [with jewels]
On which they will recline facing one another,
While around them circle immortal celestial youths
With goblets and ewers and a cup from a flowing spring,
From which they will suffer no headache nor will they
    become intoxicated.[34]

Our purpose in employing these quotations from these scriptures is to stress both the importance and the unabashed physical nature of references to this doctrine by these monotheistic religions.

From this brief description of the development of belief in the resurrection of the dead we turn to an examination of its possible meaning to a man of faith. We already have indicated that this doctrine partakes of the nature of myth—it concerns God's purpose for his faithful ones after death—and that it not only is unnecessary but is even wrong to interpret the doctrine literally. If we ask, however, what it is that belief in bodily resurrection signifies, we find somewhat the sort of meaning for one in the biblical circle of faith that rebirth has for a person in the Indian tradition. In the first place, bodily resurrection is an aspect of the belief in God as creator and as lord of one's life. The Hebrew concept of man refuses to separate soul and body, but insists that the whole man is under God's sovereignty. The rabbinical disputes over this question are extensive and fascinating, but they add up to the proposition that one cannot separate his thoughts from his actions, and one cannot separate his spiritual life from his physical life.[35] The *Shema* in Deuteronomy which Jesus repeated as the first and greatest commandment says: "You shall love the LORD your God with all your heart, and with all your soul, and with all your might." [36] This means the entire man, soul and body.

God's sovereignty over man also means that entrance into his kingdom is not an individual matter, but that the whole

[34] *Ibid.*, Sura LVI: 10-19, p. 140.
[35] Cf. Moore, *Judaism*, II., part VII, chap. III, "Eschatology."
[36] Deut. 6:5.

man, known by other whole persons, is the one who will enter into the kingdom, to be with his loved ones in a social context. The goal of life is not isolation of the individual soul as in the *moksha* (release) of Jainism, nor is it union with a World-soul as in the Hindu Upanishads. It is compared, instead, by Jesus to a great marriage feast, and by the rabbis to an eternal sabbath of feasting and rejoicing, and in the Qur'an to a happy fellowship of feasting and rest. Although Heaven is described in such physical terms, the message that God's purpose for man will not be thwarted by death is quite clear.

We already have mentioned a second meaning to be found in this doctrine. This is its value as an answer to the problem of theodicy, the biblical form of the problem of evil. Although it is obvious that God's purpose is not fulfilled in this life, and sin and death appear to triumph over good lives in many cases, in the resurrection all will be evened up if only one has faith and trusts in God's power and goodness.

The best-known aspect of this doctrine of bodily resurrection concerns the stress on physical rewards and punishments in heaven or hell. In chapter four above we discussed such eschatological sanctions and need here only emphasize that this belief in individual responsibility appears to lie at the root of the great social concern that has been so prominent in the history of the biblical faiths. This is not to ignore the terrible record of wars and persecutions which also seem to characterize these same religions, a subject we intend to discuss in the final chapter. But the concern for widows and orphans, for the sick, needy, and friendless in Judaism, Christianity, and Islam are rooted in the very same scriptures that stress the reality of the resurrection of the dead and the final judgment. In fact, it is this mixture of eschatology and ethics that appears to dominate the more prophetic aspects of the biblical religions, from Amos through Jesus and Muhammad.[37] This is made quite clear in Jesus' parable of the judgment of

[37] Cf. Amos Niven Wilder, *Eschatology and Ethics in the Teaching of Jesus* (New York: Harper & Brothers, 1939).

the Son of man, which could just as easily have been Jewish or Muslim.

Then the King will say to those at his right hand, "Come, O blessed of my Father, inherit the kingdom prepared for you from the foundation of the world; for I was hungry and you gave me food, I was thirsty and you gave me drink, I was a stranger and you welcomed me, I was naked and you clothed me, I was sick and you visited me, I was in prison and you came to me." [38]

## The Way of the Ancestors in East Asia

The religious traditions of East Asia are as complex as those of biblical lands and of India. But from the mixture of the Taoist teaching of the natural way, Confucian ancestor worship, and the infusion of Buddhism into this double stream of Chinese thought, we want to isolate the Confucian (and Japanese Shinto) stress on following the way of the ancestors. This concern to follow the way of the ancients has been sharply criticized by Christian missionaries from Europe and the United States. It has been called pagan polytheism, and some have refused to dignify the cult of the ancestors by calling it a religion.

One recent book, *Confucius and Christ: A Christian Estimate of Confucius*, by Leo Sherley-Price, in commenting on the intolerable burden of duties imposed by Confucius on the filial son, says that "the weight of the 'dead hand' weighs heavily upon his enterprises, his initiative is restrained, his desire for reform or readjustment regarded as blameworthy." [39] This is essentially the judgment returned by generations of Christians who have worked in China and studied its culture. The family loyalty which is basic to the Confucian system has resulted in many practices which are condemned by the Westerner. The nepotism rampant in pre-Communist China meant that if a man was hired to work on a project, or employed by a business firm, it was his duty, not only to get as

[38] Matt. 25:34-36.
[39] (New York: The Philosophical Library, 1951), p. 110.

many of his relatives hired as he could, but also to see that any business dealings would be shunted in their direction. The term "squeeze" is used to refer to the dribbles of money and goods that are drained from any business transaction for the benefit of relatives. What we call "graft" in our culture was apparently a way of life for public officials in the old China.

Another criticism, leveled constantly by missionaries, is against the ways in which the Chinese family system tends to debase women by placing an undue emphasis on the necessity to have sons to continue the family line. Since the basic purpose of a Confucian marriage is to propagate sons, a wife's status is contingent on whether she was able to fulfill this function.[40] The husband, for his part, is expected to take extra wives, or to procure concubines, if necessary, in order that he may have sons.

It may seem strange to discuss the doctrine of the future life in terms of ancestor worship, but there are strong biblical precedents for this. As we have said, man's views about the origins of man and his world, and also of the final end of things, must be expressed in the language of myth. In most religions there is a strong similarity between the descriptions of the beginning and the end. In the monistic thought of the Hindu Upanishads, for instance, the ocean of being, that is, the World-soul, gives rise to the universe of time and space, and after 4,320,000,000 years of existence the universe subsides again into a peaceful ocean of being. In the Bible the story of man's innocence and obedience in the Garden of Eden is paralleled with New Testament descriptions of the final kingdom of God as a state of idyllic existence in which man lives in a condition of innocence and obedience to his creator, and all nature is redeemed. Paul refers to the Christ as the "second Adam," whose obedience cancels out the first Adam's disobedience.[41] German scholars have a phrase for this which is quite succinct. They say that "Urzeit gleicht

[40] Cf. Francis L. K. Hsu, *Under the Ancestors' Shadow* (New York: Columbia University Press, 1948), chap. IV, "Continuing the Incense Smoke."
[41] Rom. 5:12-14.

167

Endzeit," the time of the beginning is just like the time of fulfillment.

In Confucian thought this possibility was carried almost to the extreme in that Confucius' goal for man was to recover the idealized past. We are again reminded that he insisted that he was not an innovator but rather was one who was attempting to transmit the best from the ancients, and that his editing and publishing of the classics was for the purpose of giving man a guide for living based on the best from the past. His twofold purpose, to develop the perfect man in a perfect society, was modeled upon the "golden age" of the sage emperors of the predynastic period. Confucius' teaching of the necessity for the rectification of names is basic to his system. This represents the conviction that if everyone were to live his life in terms of who he truly is (compare the similar advice currently offered by guidance counselors) the confusion of roles which causes students to try to act like administrators, wives to attempt to be the boss in the family, or girls to act like boys, would disappear. But in order for this to come about the ancient virtues of *hsiao* and *shu*, which were discussed in chapter four, must be inculcated and followed. Hsiao is the teaching of filial respect for his superior on the part of anyone in an inferior position. Shu is the attitude of justice and condescension with which the superior should reciprocate the hsiao which he receives.

Now just as many Hindus appear to literalize the meaning of rebirth and thus distort its real intent, and members of biblical religions sometimes carry belief in the bodily resurrection to pathological extremes, it is obvious that later admirers of Confucius emphasized his teachings on the rectification of names and filial piety out of all proportion. Under the Confucian system of education the first book studied and memorized by the pupil is the *Hsiao Ching* (the Book of Filial Piety). To this sometimes is added a collection called *The Twenty-Four Examples of Filial Duty*. It is true that the Analects often quote Confucius on the values of hsiao. Thus in Analects 11:5 we read: "Meng I Tzu asked about the treat-

168

ment of parents. The Master said, Never disobey! . . . Fan Ch'ih said, In what sense did you mean it? The Master said, While they are alive, serve them according to ritual and sacrifice to them according to ritual." But the *Hsiao Ching* makes this respect for parents practically the single, over-riding consideration as a guide for conduct, while the twenty-four examples illustrate in hair-raising detail the extremes, including facing a tiger unarmed, to which a son is expected to go in order to show his filial respect.

An even more dramatic illustration of the importance of filial piety in Confucianism is the tremendous importance given to graveyards and to the proper care of the departed ancestors by their survivors. In his careful and interesting study of a typical Chinese village, *Under the Ancestors' Shadow: Chinese Culture and Personality,* Dr. Francis L. K. Hsu has a chapter on "Worldly and Otherworldly Residences," and he begins his discussion of graveyards as follows:

There are three places of residence for members of the family who have passed away—the graveyard (or graveyards), the family shrine, and the clan temple. The graveyard is to house the bodies of dead members of the family; the other two, their spirits.

Naturally, only the richer families can afford to spend much on their graveyards, but a "good" graveyard is the concern of every family, rich or poor. The rich view their graveyards with pride; the poor look upon those of the rich with envy. Every family which has any means has a graveyard of its own. A proper graveyard is just as essential to the family as a proper house. A family which has to entomb its dead in a public graveyard is an object of pity.[42]

If we turn our attention, however, from the bizarre and the extreme in the Confucian cult of the ancestors, and ask instead what it means in a positive way, what value it has to a follower of Confucius, what can be said? In this circle of faith it appears that concern for the way of the ancestors has much the same value that we found for the two doctrines discussed earlier in the Indian and the biblical circles of faith. Let us examine the Confucian tradition in terms of the same three considerations, the doctrine of man, the problem of evil, and the motivation for ethical living.

Although Confucius taught that man is born good, and that he should be taught the virtues which characterized the life of the ancient worthies, this teaching must be given some clear content in order for man to know what exactly it is that constitutes virtuous living. In biblical religions a similar problem exists. One is expected to obey the will of God to be a righteous man, but the question must still be answered: What is the will of God? In the Bible various religious leaders gave various answers. The priest, the prophet, and the wiseman of Israel, each stressed in turn the Law, the Word of God, and Wisdom as definitive for God's will for man. In the New Testament the ethical teachings of Jesus were used to instruct the convert in proper conduct. In Hinduism one is expected to live a virtuous life according to his birth, to follow the dharma for his class. But this duty must first be defined, and such writings as the Laws of Manu were produced for this purpose. So too with the followers of Confucius. In their case the definition of the virtuous life came to be defined especially in terms of the Hsiao Ching. The first chapter of this classic has Confucius say, among other things:

The duty of children to their parents is the fountain whence all other virtues spring, and also the starting-point from which we ought to begin our education. . . . Our body and hair and skin are all derived from our parents, and therefore we have no right to injure any of them in the least. This is the first duty of a child. . . .

The first duty of a son is to pay a careful attention to every want of his parents. The next is to serve his government loyally; and the last to establish a good name for himself.

So it is written in the Ta Ya: "You must think of your ancestors and continue to cultivate the virtue which you inherit from them." [43]

[43] Ivan Chen, tr., *The Book of Filial Duty* (translated from the Chinese of the *Hsiao Ching*) (London: John Murray, 1920), pp. 16-17.

In the context of the belief that man is born good, there-fore, the Confucian gentleman is expected to follow a pattern of life which elevates the requirements of obedience to parents and family loyalty above the five virtues of Confucian thought. Although this led to a loss of much of the dynamic of the Master's original message, it did help develop the tremendous sense of continuity which is so important in Confucianism. The past and the present and the future are all bound together by this stress on filial duty.

This leads us to a comment on Confucian influence in Japan. In chapter three we pointed out that in Confucian thought man's troubles, such as war, famine, and disease, could be traced to lack of harmony in the world, caused by failure to follow the ancients and to inculcate filial piety. In Japan, where Confucian morality was the main source of ethics, the teaching of hsiao became even stronger in application and practice. Loyalty to the emperor was carried to fanatical ex-tremes, and one's sense of duty to his ancestors and family gave rise to such an interesting custom as hara-kiri, suicide by disembowelment. In many cases resort to hara-kiri, and in more recent times other forms of suicide, is determined by the re-morse of a person who feels that he has failed his parents and his nation in some way. Suicide becomes then the ultimate expression of hsiao since it demonstrates the sincerity of the unfortunate victim. A more positive form of this same suicide pattern was, of course, often demonstrated in World War II, when Kamikaze pilots (named for the "divine wind" which destroyed a Chinese fleet on its way to invade Japan in the thirteenth century) gave their all in loyalty to the nation.

Finally, in the area of Confucian conduct, what often ap-pears to the outsider as unethical behavior is often simply the carrying out of the logic of hsiao. The "squeeze" and the nepotism associated with the business practices of the Chinese are of course part of the system of family loyalty. I well re-member hearing about the Tong wars in the Chinatowns of California when I was young, and then, later on, my great surprise when I read sociological discussions of the very low

171

crime rate in these same Chinatowns. It turned out that the Tong wars (of Taoist secret society origin) were between family groups, but that the Confucian family system, with its demands of hsiao, kept juvenile delinquency, murder, theft, and rape to an almost irreducible minimum.

Much more could be written about the future life as illustrative of the differences between the major and minor circles of faith. There would, as for the other areas of life, appear to be major differences between the discernible patterns of thought and behavior. The belief in rebirth does much to undergird the ancient class system of India and to determine the way of life for millions of Jains and Buddhists. The biblical belief in the resurrection of the body testifies to the conviction that the God of the Bible is Lord of history and will redeem his creation in its entirety. The Confucian concern for the way of the ancients and the desire on the part of the Chinese and Japanese to become ancestors worthy to be remembered by their posterity have been most influential in all of East Asia. Each of these three forms of belief about future life is in harmony with other tenets in its circle of faith, but they also appear to be mutually exclusive, one of the other.

CHAPTER 7

# GO YE INTO
# ALL THE WORLD

Perhaps the most significant factor which differentiates the world's religions is that only a few are missionary in nature, whereas the majority are not. In this chapter we will analyze, in relation to our thesis of circles of faith, the missionary dynamics of the three great missionary religions, Buddhism, Christianity, and Islam. But first a word is in order concerning some of those religions which have either failed to develop, or at least to maintain, a missionary program.

Of the several elements which appear to be necessary for a religion to have a worldwide mission, the most important is that its message be universal, both in its appeal and its inclusive nature. This means that there must be no human restrictions such as birth, sex, or color in its message to the world, but that the religion must be open to all who are willing to respond to its call to salvation. Let us examine briefly several nonmissionary religions from this aspect of universalism.

Hinduism has experienced missionary expansion in past centuries into Southeast Asia and Indonesia, and in this century through such a movement in Europe and the Americas

173

as the Ramakrishna Mission. In spite of such important exceptions, however, Hinduism remains basically a nonmissionary religion. This is due, at least in part, to the Hindu assumption that one's birth into this world was caused by past karma which has predestined one's fate in this present life. One's social and religious duty is determined by the class (*jati*, birth) into which one is born, so that a man is superior to a woman, and a Brahman is superior to a Kshatriya, Vaisya, or Shudra. In orthodox Brahmanism, therefore, the three lower classes are doomed to further rebirths before final nirvana may be reached, and in this life each of the lower classes is expected to give religious honor and service to those in a higher class. All non-Hindus, also, are automatically classed as "outcaste," born outside the structure of Hindu dharma, so that technically a European, for instance, cannot actually become a Hindu, for the only true Hindu is one who was born into the Hindu social structure. Even *bhakti-marga*, the way of salvation by faith in a savior god who offers present hope and future peace to those in the lower classes, can be followed only within the context of Hinduism.

In East Asia Confucianism and Shinto are two other religions which lack this element of universality. The way of life advocated by Confucius presupposed the social structure of ancient China. He sought to develop the ideal man in a society patterned on the ancient feudal structure. In Japan the Shinto teaching of *kami*, the notion that everything Japanese —the islands of Japan, the people, the animals, and even the mountains—is kami, or holy, presupposes on the negative side that the rest of the world is not kami. The Japanese term for this indigenous religion, *kami no michi*, the way of the kami, or gods, is illustrative of the presupposition that the Japanese people uniquely are directly descended from the gods. For such reasons neither Confucianism nor Shinto has ever had a true missionary message.

In the first century of the Christian era Judaism had a vigorous and appealing missionary movement. It has been demonstrated that much of the early, almost miraculous spread of Christianity followed Jewish missionary methods, and that the new religion also siphoned off a large number of Diaspora Jews. Judaism's message of one true God for all men, and its call to an ethical life, had wide appeal. But after Christianity had become the dominant religion it proscribed Judaism and for various reasons, including Christian persecution, the Jewish missionary movement withered. Today Judaism tends to be identified with a cultural expression of Talmudic teachings and, with rare exceptions, members of this faith have become so by virtue of being born of Jewish parents.

What makes a religion missionary? Of the three elements which historians have found to be essential the one of universality already has been discussed, at least negatively. In the positive sense universality means that a religion, to be truly missionary, must have a message which says in effect: O man! whoever you are, and whatever your station in life, we offer you help, purpose, and fulfillment. Nothing that has happened to you in the past, neither birth, evil deed, nor any other condition bars you from the true way of salvation. All men stand equal, both in need of the salvation we preach and also in their right to receive it without hindrance from any other person.

Though the message of a missionary religion must be universal in its appeal, this is not enough. It must, in the second place, possess a high degree of continuity which will enable it to endure for centuries without too much change. Without roots in the past and continuing central traditions and practices which lend stability and continuity to the movement it might dissipate, or possibly become fragmented, or at least suffer such radical change that it would cease to bear any resemblance to the original movement. There must be certain things held in common, for instance, by a Buddhist in first-century Ceylon, tenth-century China, and twentieth-century London for each to be called "Buddhist."

The third ingredient, which we will call adaptability, means that the movement must be flexible enough to adapt to new times, areas, and conditions. Jainism in India, and Shinto in Japan, for instance, are "stay-at-home" religions which would

175

be greatly out of place in alien cultures. Buddhism and Christianity, on the other hand, seem to be able to adapt to new situations readily enough to enable them to become worldwide. The message of each is truly universal in that its appeal is relevant to men in many different cultures and climes.

## Buddhism as a Missionary Religion

Twenty-five hundred years after the death of Gautama, the Buddha, the religion which he began is the most influential in East Asia. Its leaders claim some 160 million members, although Buddhism does not keep records or statistics, and thus any figure is an estimate. It is certain that in addition to these active practitioners of the Way of the Buddha the lives of 500 million Asians are directly influenced by Buddhism, and another half billion breathe the air of the Buddhist world view. Yet in India, the land of Buddhism's origins, the religion's adherents (until very recently) have numbered in the hundreds of thousands, rather than in the millions. How can we explain the amazing growth and influence of Buddhism throughout South and East Asia, and at the same time account for its rapid spread, but eventual subsidence in India?

It is a paradox that the Buddha, who taught salvation by severing of all attachments to this world, should also be responsible for inaugurating a vigorous missionary religion. This paradox is dealt with in the myth of Gautama's temptation by Mara, the Evil One. At the time of his Enlightenment Mara, that is, "Death," tried to dissuade him from his resolve to share his hard-won Truth with mankind. Mara pointed out that, since this Buddha knowledge called for one to have no desires or attachments of any kind, Gautama should have no desire to help others, and if he did he might risk losing his own salvation. But the Lord Buddha, in his infinite compassion, resolved to teach the Path to all who would listen. His resolve was vindicated both by the response which his message received and also by the subsequent experience of Buddhist

176

converts, which convinced them that the spreading of the Doctrine was not incompatible with the Four Noble Truths.

An early legend relates that after the first sixty-one converts had joined the movement the Lord Buddha sent them out with the following charge:

And the Blessed One said to the Bhikkhus: "I am delivered, O Bhikkhus, from all fetters, human and divine. You, O Bhikkhus, are also delivered from all fetters, human and divine. Go ye now, O Bhikkhus, and wander, for the gain of the many, for the welfare of the many, out of compassion for the world, for the good, for the gain, and for the welfare of gods and men. Let not two of you go the same way. Preach, O Bhikkhus, the doctrine which is glorious in the beginning, glorious in the middle, glorious at the end, in the spirit and in the letter; proclaim a consummate, perfect, and pure life of holiness. There are beings whose mental eyes are covered by scarcely any dust, but if the doctrine is not preached to them, they cannot attain salvation. They will understand the doctrine. And I will go also, O Bhikkhus, to Uruvelâ, to Senâninigama, in order to preach the doctrine." [1]

During the forty-five years that remained of his life the Buddha preached and taught his Truth, and by the time of his death the Sangha, or Order, was well developed. What was there about his message that caused followers to flock to this new movement, especially when the convert had to renounce completely his normal way of life—family, friends, and livelihood? In its simplest form the explanation probably has two main facets. The first of these would be the universal nature of the invitation to salvation. As noted in chapter five, Gautama lived in an age of radical social change in which a sense of individual insecurity resulted from the uprooting of established patterns of political and social life. But a more important basis for this universal appeal stemmed from Hindu beliefs concerning class distinctions, which doomed all persons born below the level of the Brahman class to further re-

[1] *Vinaya Texts, The Mahāvagga,* I:11, tr. from the Pali by T. W. Rhys Davids and Hermann Oldenberg. Sacred Books of the East, XIII (London: Oxford University Press, 1881), 112.

births. The Buddha offered the promise of salvation to anyone in this present existence. Members of each and every class were acceptable to the Order, and even the prostitute and murderer were given new hope. Just as in our day many depressed groups of Asia and Africa are attracted to communism because it offers them new hope, telling them that they "have nothing to lose but their chains," so many in sixth-century B.C. India must have turned to Buddhism with new hope.

The other aspect of the movement which helped launch it strongly on its way was undoubtedly the actual experience of freedom, of bliss, of release which thousands of converts experienced. The literature is full of devout and exultant expressions of joy and peace which reflect the sense of new meaning which entered the lives of new converts. With salvation offered to all rather than only to select groups, and with many witnesses to the truth of the new doctrine, the movement spread rapidly.

Two limitations upon its missionary impetus, however, were the rigid demands of the new order and the placing of women in a lesser role than men. The vows of poverty and chastity and the requirement that the monk must seek his livelihood by begging were stringent demands. This was partially softened by the development of a strong lay movement. Those who were unwilling or felt themselves to be unable to seek final nirvana at the end of this existence could improve their situation in a future existence by giving liberal alms to the mendicant monks, and gifts of land and money to the Order itself. This made possible the expansion of the Order, for otherwise the Indian communities would soon have been overburdened by the large number of beggars. A favorite theme in the Buddhist devotional literature is the recounted stories of the tremendous benefits accruing, both in present and future lives, to those who might offer as little as a cup of water to a monk.

The tradition that women are spiritually inferior to men goes back to Gautama himself, and some early teachings imply that for any being (animal, human female, a god, a tree) to achieve final deliverance it must first be reborn as a human

178

male, so that by implication it would be rare for a woman to achieve final nirvana at the end of her present life. In any case the Buddha is reported to have admitted women to an order of nuns (*bhikkhunis*), but only grudgingly and after much urging from the disciple Ananda. This reluctance appears to be linked partly with the problem, obviously a serious one, raised by the requirement of chastity and pure thoughts. The problem of the human sexual drive appears to have been regarded by the Buddha as one of the most difficult forms of desire to eliminate. One early rule which is expected to be applied even in our day, when we have large hotels, is that no monk be permitted to sleep in the same building (under the same roof) as a nun. The women who become nuns must experience the humiliation of being required to take eight special vows, each of which subordinates the nun to the monk. Thus the first of these rules goes: "A nun even of a hundred years' standing shall (first) salute a monk and rise up before him, even if he is only just ordained." [2] Even though this attitude toward women appears to be a spiritual carryover from Hinduism and is inconsistent with the basic message of Buddhism, it does remain as a limitation on the universalism of early Buddhism.

By the time of the death of the Buddha those aspects of Buddhism which were to give it continuity as a missionary religion were well developed. From earliest times down to the present day anyone who desires to enter into the Buddhist way of salvation and become a monk or a nun makes a three-fold declaration: "I go for refuge to the Buddha; I go for refuge to the Dhamma (teaching); I go for refuge to the Sangha (Order)." Even though there exist wide differences across the world of Buddhism as to the nature of the person of the Buddha, and disagreement over what is important in the Dhamma, or the sort of discipline demanded by various units of the Sangha, the "three jewels," as the three refuges are called, represent a common denominator for all Buddhist

[2] E. J. Thomas, *The Life of the Buddha as Legend and History* (New York: Columbia University Press, 1927) p. 108.

monks. Thus Gautama, the Buddha, whose entrance into nirvana occurred about twenty-five hundred years ago, is the spiritual head of the religion. The basic teachings of Buddhism are those found in the Pali canon, the *Tripitaka*, or "three baskets" of teachings, which are known everywhere in South and East Asia. And the Sanghas, which are widely spread, represent refuges where one can go when he leaves the world in order to follow the Way, based upon the Four Noble Truths and the Noble Eightfold Path. This core of common tradition gives Buddhists much in common, and in spite of the many forms, some of them weird, which Buddhism has taken, these cannot be lacking and still remain Buddhism.

The element of adaptability, which we have indicated as the third necessary ingredient of a missionary religion, has at times been almost too free in Buddhism. This religion grew out of the Hinduism of its day and was, in its primitive form, not too different from certain other expressions of Hinduism. Though it tended to deny the teaching of class distinctions, in principle it did not fight this position actively. Thus Basham points out that "membership of the Buddhist Order was not restricted by caste, but slaves, soldiers, debtors, and other persons under obligation or in tutelage might not enter it without the permission of their superior." [3] In other words, Buddhism called upon one to make a radical break with society but it did not call upon society itself to change radically. And it refused to be a refuge for those who simply were disgruntled with their present lot.

In a much wider sense Buddhism has proved itself to be uninterested in cultural or social change of any thoroughgoing sort. Perhaps this is because of its presupposition that this present life is but one of many possible existences in a world which is itself actually unimportant. Buddhist tolerance, for instance, seems to say in effect: "Start where you are to become enlightened. If in this present life you are willing and able to start on the hard path, well and good. If you believe

[3] *The Wonder That Was India*, p. 281.

and act otherwise, that too is all right, for you will have many more chances in future lives. Remember that in the end every sentient being will achieve nirvana."

In practice this tolerant attitude has meant that little attention is paid to the social context out of which people are called to enter upon the Way. Christian missionaries have commented that the Burmese farmer is apt to be more concerned with the Nats—the local spirits of the soil—than with the teachings of the Buddha. In China or Ceylon, in Tibet, or back-country Japan, primitive practices and beliefs can be found right alongside a Buddhist monastery. Buddhism flows over a culture and sinks into the interstices of social custom with little shock to the society. Though persecution in India and China against Buddhists has occurred off and on across the centuries, it seldom, if ever, has been because the Buddhists wanted to change the order of things. Rather it was for such reasons as objection to the way in which the Buddhist call to renounce the world broke up family patterns, or because the greed of rulers was aroused by the increasing wealth of the monasteries.

In fact, it was for reasons such as these that Buddhism, which at one time dominated most of North India, gradually began to lose ground to resurgent Hinduism and finally almost disappeared from the Indian scene until recent decades. The challenge of the universalism of Buddhism to the class and caste structure of Hinduism was met by the rise of the bhakti cults of Vishnu and Shiva. These also began to offer salvation to anyone, even those of low birth, who turned to the deity in faith and trust. At the same time the monastic organization of Buddhism meant that over the centuries the various Sanghas accumulated vast amounts of land and wealth, so that when the Muslim invaders began to infiltrate Northwest India in the eighth century this concentration of property formed natural targets for conquest. The breaking up of the monasteries meant, in turn, the gradual dissolution of the strength of Buddhism centered in the Sangha.

Outside of India, however, the story is somewhat different.

With these three elements of the universality of its message of salvation, the three jewels of refuge, and the aspect of tolerant adaptability to give it a missionary impetus, how has Buddhism fared in history? Although this religion, because of its complex nature, has been called a family of religions, which makes it difficult to categorize, there are two main branches of Buddhism which have distinctive messages. These are the Buddhism of the Elders, called Theravada, found in South Asia, and the Mahayana, or great vehicle, found in Central and East Asia.

The School of Theravada Buddhism claims to be closer to the original teachings of the Buddha than the Mahayana. It is strong in Ceylon, Burma, and Southeast Asia. Its stress is upon following Gautama as a spiritual guide and upon rigorous following of the Dhamma. The monk often serves as a teacher of the young and as spiritual leader in the community. Stress is upon denial of the way of the world in order to achieve enlightenment. Because of its narrow concern with self-salvation, it is sometimes called Hinayana, the "lesser vehicle, or doctrine," by the Mahayana Buddhists.

The real missionary dynamic of Buddhism is found in the teachings of the Mahayana. This form of the religion is dominant in Tibet, Mongolia, China, Korea, and Japan. Two specific emphases of the Mahayana appear to strengthen its missionary appeal. The first of these is the development of the concept of the Bodhisattva. This is the teaching that the historical Buddha, and other enlightened beings as well, have achieved the right to enter nirvana. But out of love for mankind (much as Gautama resolved to share his teaching with mankind) these beings have resolved not to enter nirvana, but rather to remain in contact with the world of men. The tremendous merit which these beings have piled up permits them to make a surplus available to aid those who call upon them by faith. As indicated in chapter three, this makes it possible for one to marry, have children, and live a normal life, yet still hope to enter nirvana at death. Many Mahayana Buddhists still become monks or nuns, for although this is not considered necessary to salvation it is considered to be meritorious. There is some parallel here with the Roman Catholic teaching of the merit of the saints which is available through prayer, but it is closer to polytheism and magical religion in practice. Thus in China, the Ch'ing T'u (pure land) sect teaches the complete efficacy for salvation merely of repeating the name of a Bodhisattva, "Amitabha" (unmeasured light)—in Japan this becomes the repetition of the name "Omitofu"—while Kwang Yin, the Goddess of Mercy, is worshiped as a Bodhisattva. In Japan, especially, this phenomenon makes possible the rise of mass movements under strong leadership and the constant division of Buddhism into new sects and movements.

The second impetus in Mahayana is the development of the concept of nirvana into a positive view of life after death. In chapter six we saw that, although the Buddha was agnostic on the subject of what nirvana was, his later followers were not content to leave the subject there. Hinayana has made some contributions to a positive statement of the hope of nirvana, but in Mahayana the concept of nirvana is turned into a specific hope for heaven and fear of hell. The history of religion tends to support the probability that such a philosophical abstraction as "nirvana as emptiness" either has no appeal to the average person or else is incomprehensible to him. The Mahayana success in mass appeal, as opposed to the limited results of the Hinayana, in this matter of the future life is further documentation for this probability. Thus we have the ironic situation of hundreds of millions of Buddhists accepting doctrines which would appear to be contradictory to their founder's teachings. If the Buddha taught that there is no god who can help man on his path to nirvana, and also that nirvana is not to be described in any positive way, the Hinayana Buddhists may be right in claiming to be closer to the original teachings of the historical Gautama. But they have not had the numerical success of the Mahayana.

What, in summary, can we say concerning our evaluation of Buddhism as a missionary religion? Its message of salvation has for our day the same universality it has always had. The modern American could well find in Buddhism surcease from anxiety which is now sought in alcohol, tranquilizers, and the psychiatrist's couch. In Asia, where life is burdensome, the life span is short, and hunger and back-breaking toil are the average lot, the Buddhist view of life has strong appeal. The religion also has a strong line of continuity in the Buddha, Dhamma, and Sangha. In adaptability it would appear to be too lenient, since in India, for instance, the rise of Hindu savior cults and, later on, the Muslim invasions practically erased the religion from the land of its birth.

In the light of developments since World War II, however, such easy generalizations from history must be carefully hedged about with all sorts of qualifications. For history does show that, very often, pressures and persecutions which threaten a religion evoke new vigor and lead to patterns of change which enable the movement to survive as it adapts. The Hinayana teaching, "to exist is to suffer," seems to be in sharp contradiction to the world-affirming doctrines of modern science, technology, Marxism, and Western technology. Yet in the new nations arising out of the ruins of colonialism there is found everywhere the desire to base their search for identity on indigenous traditions. Buddhism, which is identified with so many of the cultures of South and East Asia, is a natural grass-roots tradition around which to rally the loyalties of the citizens.

Although nationalism is the great enemy of any international movement, whether it be the League of Nations, the United Nations, ecumenical Buddhism, Christianity, Islam, and also, it should be added, communism, it also often is responsible for calling out strong loyalties in unexpected ways.

Perhaps this is one reason why the unexpected is happening in the world of Buddhism. Recently in Ceylon the Buddhist monks led a political movement to prevent a Communist takeover. In Saigon the political associations of recent Buddhist suicides by burning have been obvious, especially in view of the Buddhist abhorrence of suicide under usual circumstances.

184

In India, the land of its birth, Buddhism which so long had lain dormant is experiencing new vigor and in recent years, as the lower classes seek freedom from the Hindu social structure, surprisingly has received several million new converts. In view of such developments and its renewed vigor in Japan and other countries, including the United States, it is not possible to predict the future of this oldest of the missionary religions.

## Christianity as a Missionary Religion

The religion which arose around the person of Jesus, the Christ, claims over 900 million followers spread around the globe. The areas of greatest concentration of this faith are Europe, North and South America, and such British colonial areas as Australia and South Africa. There are three main branches of Christianity, the Eastern Orthodox centered in southeastern Europe, the Roman Catholic, with strong centers in southern Europe and North and South America, and Protestantism, with strong centers in northern Europe, North America, and Australia. Each division has taken a different approach in the area of missions, of which the most dramatic has been the missionary program of North American Protestantism begun in the nineteenth century, probably the most vigorous missionary program of all history.

The career of Jesus was quite short, for after a ministry of a year or two he was executed by the Roman government in Palestine. As we have seen in chapter five, the earliest Christian communities grew up among those who believed that the God of the Jews had raised Jesus from the dead. This resurrection was the basis for the claim that he was the long-awaited Jewish Messiah, or Christ. Even before our earliest sources were written this claim was strengthened by identifying Jesus also as the risen Lord (kurios) who represented not only the fulfillment of God's promise to send a Messiah to rescue his people, but also the Hellenistic notion of a savior god who had power over death. By raising Jesus from the grave God

185

showed his power over death, and it was believed that those who trusted in Jesus as risen Lord could also share in God's victory over death. Thus in the man Jesus were combined the claim that he represented the final revelation of the ancient Jewish God, the ethical purpose and demands of Judaism, and the appeal of the promise of immortality by faith in a savior god found in the Greek mystery religions.

The universalism of Christianity was shown, in the first place, by the fact that almost from the beginning it offered salvation to anyone who was willing to meet its requirements. It did not matter what one's station in life was, nor was there any barrier based on sex, slavery, race, or criminal record. At one point, however, there is ambiguity in the early record. Although the apostle Paul states that in Christ "there is neither male nor female," [4] he also laid down the rule to the Corinthians: "As in all the churches of the saints, the women should keep silence in the churches. For they are not permitted to speak, but should be subordinate, as even the law says." [5]

It is true that in Christianity, almost from the beginning, women have held a subordinate position both in church office and also in the social customs of most Christian communities. The Papacy and the Roman Catholic hierarchy are dominated by men, and most Protestant clerical orders either exclude women or place them in a subordinate role. It would appear, however, that this tradition of female inferiority is not inherent in the gospel message, but is instead a cultural factor, like the same phenomenon in Buddhism, which is almost worldwide, perhaps because throughout history religious traditions have been almost entirely in the control of men.

What did the early church require of those seeking admission to its ranks? Here we can see the universality of Christianity in terms of its appeal to the needs and interests of its early hearers. It offered hope to anyone who felt the need of help to live in that first-century world with its many frighten-

[4] Gal. 3:28.
[5] I Cor. 14:33-34.

ing aspects, and also replaced the fear of death with a promise of life beyond the grave. The requirements were neither exclusive nor difficult. To join the Christian fellowship it was necessary that one affirm faith in Jesus as Christ and risen Lord. This meant that one held the conviction that the God of the Jews truly had revealed his purpose in history and had demonstrated that he was Lord of life by raising his Son from the dead. This faith had two important corollaries: To own Jesus as risen Lord meant, first of all, that one must obey him in terms of ethical living. This obedience, in the second place, was both verified and made possible by the experience of receiving the gift of God's Holy Spirit. Just as a Buddhist convert might receive a foretaste of the bliss of nirvana by experiencing the cooling of his desires, so the Christian convert experienced God's power at work in his life, a power which was expected to produce the "fruits" of ethical living and of Christian brotherly love. Thus faith in Jesus led to a life of love expressed in present ethical living and carried with it the hope of a new life after death as the gift of God's power.

One reason why Christianity won out over its many rivals in its appeal to men's loyalties was the high degree of continuity which it possessed. As the early Christians sought to share their gift of salvation with others, and the movement spread, there was the constant danger that the movement might become fragmented. But several things have always been held in common by all Christians. The first of these is the man Jesus. None of the Greek mystery religions with which Christianity competed had a person such as Jesus around whom to center their story of salvation. In the second place, Jesus and all his disciples were Jews who brought into Christianity their heritage of the Jewish scriptures. As the church grew in size and began to create its own literature the New Testament was added to the Old Testament to form the Bible, which served as the common Scripture for the movement. Finally, there is the Christian church itself, which in spite of its many schisms represents a common fellowship of believers who own the Lordship of Christ, have in common the Bible, and, at least in most cases, share in the use of the sacraments. Thus instead of the Buddha, the Dhamma, and the Sangha we have the parallel of the Christ, the Bible, and the church. Around these three have revolved the different interpretations of Christianity which eventually produced the three main divisions of the church and the many sects.

What of the ability of Christianity to adapt itself to new places and times? This history is a mixed bag with much in it to be praised and much to be criticized or blamed. The original gospel message was not identified with any culture but was instead a representation of God's judgment upon any and every human achievement. Jesus' ethical teachings are peculiarly free from social legislation which could be used as a basis for a particular social pattern. Thus he did not, or else refused to, say whether Christians should permit divorce, pay the tax to Caesar, or follow any other human tradition. Instead, he pointed always and firmly to God's will and to the principle of following God's way rather than man's way. Although the apostle Paul wrote to the Roman Christians that they should "be subject to the governing authorities," [6] it was this same Roman government which executed him. Paul's prudential concern to keep the church from any conflict which might destroy it is to be balanced by the command: "Do not be conformed to this world but be transformed by the renewal of your mind, that you may prove what is the will of God, what is good and acceptable and perfect." [7]

Christianity always has been able to adapt itself to new situations but real problems have arisen whenever Christianity has attempted to alter, or even "radically displace," its new environment with a new ethical orientation. Polytheism, polygamy, debauchery, despotism, and economic and social oppression appear always to have been natural targets for the missionary in any new cultural situation. Beginning with the call to forsake the present world as doomed and to join the

[6] Rom. 13:1.
[7] Rom. 12:2.

fellowship of Christ, this fellowship in turn seeks to redeem its environment.

This new life in faith and fellowship has led historically to many dramatic changes in society. It probably should be credited with helping some of the advances in recent history toward elimination of slavery, and also for the high measure of freedom and opportunity that women enjoy in the countries which are largely Christian. Many primitive peoples also have been transformed by missionary programs of education, from savagery to civilized society, sometimes in a matter of decades. On the other hand, when Christianity has sought to compete with such ancient and sophisticated cultures as those of India and China, it has been a different story. In India most converts have been among the primitive jungle tribes or from outcaste groups—not from the Brahman or Kshatriya castes. After almost two millennia in India[8] the Christian population is still only about 1.5 percent of the total. Why is this so?

The answer lies, at least in part, in the nature of the Christian proclamation. Whereas Buddhism teaches that each sentient being will someday achieve Buddhahood, the Christian message is one which demands decision. This one present life is one's only opportunity to determine his eternal destiny. The choice is between life and death, heaven and hell, and the decision is final. Although many would dispute whether this statement accurately reflects the gospel message, historically it is what has been taught and has been based on both the Gospel record and the rest of the New Testament. Picture the poignant tragedy of a young Hindu boy who attends a mission school and learns that his salvation rests upon his decision for Christ. His father believes, on the other hand, that if his son becomes a Christian he must suffer through many hells before being born once again into this world, after which he must again seek to raise his lot in the class structure. For the son to become a Christian represents to the father a fate worse than death for his son. So, as one report tells it,

[8] This is, of course, in reference to the claim of the Church of South India to have been founded by St. Thomas in the first Christian century.

189

such a son visited his father at home and told him that the next day he was going to accept the Christian faith, and go to live at the mission. That night the boy awoke to see his father standing over him with a knife, about to plunge it into his son's heart. In this case the boy managed to escape, and returned to the mission to tell his story. But if I were a Brahman Hindu I am certain that I would think long and hard before I jeopardized my hard-won high level of existence to enter a circle of faith considered anathema by my tradition.

Of the three main branches of Christianity the two which have been most active in recent centuries in the missionary enterprise are the Roman Catholic Church and the Protestant denominations. In a general way the record of each group has had a distinctive emphasis. The Catholic approach has tended to start at the level of the people that it is seeking to win over to the faith. Perhaps this has taken the form, as in Mexico, of baptizing the local deities into the faith. Thus the Virgin of Guadalupe is identified with the Virgin Mary. Local deities might be accepted as Christian saints and certain fertility rites brought under the practice of the church. This certainly reduces the traumatic break with the past which has tended to characterize the Protestant approach. For instance, Protestant missionaries dressed the half-naked South Sea Islanders in "Mother Hubbard" dresses; medical reports show that this additional attire was a prime cause of tuberculosis among the women. But at least the prudish missionaries were no longer offended by naked breasts.

One other limitation in the adaptability of the Christian mission lies in the long history of doctrinal dispute. When a convert responds to the good news about a God who loves him and is offered forgiveness and fellowship, but then is confronted with quarrels over the nature of the Godhead, infant baptism, and the burial of a suicide, the impact of the gospel message is blunted. In explaining why early Islam spread so rapidly among the people of Syria, Levy says: the villagers and the country folk flocked to Islam, for "although they professed Christianity, they had never properly assimilated its doctrines, and the bitter quarrels of rival churches over mystical teachings which the peasants found impossible of comprehension drove them into the arms of the invading Muslims." [9]

We find then that Christianity has in varied measure a message of universal salvation, a strong degree of continuity in Jesus the Christ, the Bible, and the church, and has proved adaptable enough to spread and establish itself in many parts of the world. At present its two greatest hurdles to further growth appear to be its uncompromising demand of a choice and break with the past on the part of new converts and its label as "the white man's religion."

Two major developments in Christianity since World War II should be noted here. The first is the manner in which Christianity has been placed on the defensive, not only in Asia and Africa where the bitterness of anticolonialism often has made Christian missions its prime target, but also in nominally Christian countries where secularism, communism, nationalism, and the scientific outlook are rapidly replacing orthodox Christian attitudes and mores at every level of life. The other noteworthy development is the great interest and activity centering in the possibility, even the necessity, of rapprochement and union between the various major and minor divisions of Christianity. It is ironical that such movements toward Christian unity, at least in part, have arisen from the necessity for Christians to close ranks in order to salvage as much of their prestige and influence as possible. At the same time it is to be hoped that much goodwill may come from this tendency toward cooperation and union.

### Islam as a Missionary Religion

The youngest of the missionary religions, and the strong rival to Christianity, is Islam. This religion was begun by the prophetic ministry of Muhammad, the Messenger of Allah.

[9] Reuben Levy, *The Social Structure of Islam* (New York: Cambridge University Press, 1957), p. 6.

Although the religion often is called Muhammadanism, members of this faith prefer the term "Islam" (submission) because they do not want to be thought of as revering the prophet as divine, as they claim the Christians have done with Jesus Christ. In the seventh century of the Christian era Islam erupted with explosive vigor out of the Arabian Peninsula, and rapidly became the dominant religion in areas formerly under Christian and Zoroastrian influence. Although Constantinople, the capital of Eastern Christendom, did not fall to the Muslims until 1453, long before this Islam controlled a wide belt of territory eastward from Morocco and Spain into Northwest India. By the fourteenth century Muslim traders and missionaries had spread their faith into Indonesia, and by the sixteenth century they had reached the Philippine Islands, only a few decades ahead of the Spanish Christians.

Islam was far more influential in the shaping of the Western tradition than the usual history of Europe would indicate. One of the major reasons for the voyages of the early explorers was to find a way around the Muslim lands of North Africa and the Near East, which until as recently as the time of Napoleon blocked direct access to India and East Asia. In fact, Southeast Europe, especially the Balkan countries, including Greece, was under the rule of the Ottoman Empire until the close of World War I. Not only were Christian countries ruled by Muslims, but many aspects of medieval Roman Catholic theology, as well as the theology of the Eastern Church, were strongly influenced by apologetic debate with Muslim intellectuals. One of the intriguing aspects of the relationships between Christians and Muslims is that, although many millions of Christians have been converted to Islam, it appears to be most difficult for Christian missionaries to convert Muslims. Thus the Dutch in Indonesia and the Spanish in the Philippines had poor results in their missionary endeavors, while in the South Sea Islands, which remained unaffected by Islam, the Christian mission has had some of its most dramatic successes.

Today there are well over four hundred million Muslims in

the world (they continue to include about one-seventh of the world's population), and two of the world's ten most populated countries are Muslim—Indonesia and Pakistan. The importance and influence of the religion are as strong today as at any time since Columbus, and it is experiencing a renaissance that is closely linked with the rising prestige in the world political scene of the new Muslim states of Africa and Asia.

In previous chapters we have discussed such aspects of Islam as its view of deity, its message of salvation, ethical living, the career of the prophet Muhammad, and Muslim eschatology—the doctrine of Allah's last day. With a minimum of repetition let us summarize the missionary dynamics of Islam with stress on the universal nature of its message, its continuity, both in time and space, and its ability to adapt to new cultures and climes.

A striking characteristic of Islam is the forceful simplicity of its beliefs and practices. Islam began in a semibarbaric area, even though Mecca and Medina were genuine cities with a good degree of urban sophistication. For instance, Arabic literature really begins with the Qur'an, and the great majority of the first converts must have been illiterate. Throughout its history Islam has had a high degree of success with uncivilized and primitive peoples, and it is claimed that one can grasp the essentials of the religion very quickly. Across the world of Islam when the *Muezzin* (he who announces) gives the call to prayer the words that float down from the *minaret* (lighthouse) repeat this message:

Allah is most great! I testify that there is no God but Allah; I testify that Muhammad is the Apostle of Allah; Come to prayer; Come to salvation: Allah is most great; There is no God but Allah! [10]

As the messenger of Allah to all mankind, Muhammad was sent as a warner to prepare men for Allah's final judgment by calling them to repentance and submission to the will of

[10] Cf. Kenneth Cragg, *The Call of the Minaret* (New York: Oxford University Press, 1956), p. 30.

Allah. As we found true for Buddhism and Christianity, it soon became necessary to move beyond this simple call to obedience to Allah and to make available to the convert a summary of the contents of Muhammad's message. From the early days of Islam has come the summary of beliefs and practices known as the Five Doctrines of the Creed and the Five Pillars of the Faith. These have served to define the nature of Muslim belief and also to unify the members of the faith in a manner that is unique in religious history.

The five beliefs to which all Muslims must give assent are not found listed as such in the Qur'an, nor in the early Hadith (tradition), but seem to have been formulated perhaps for the same reasons as the Apostles' Creed of Christianity, i.e., to enable the Muslim community to define orthodox belief and to control heretical tendencies. We have already listed the doctrines and the duties of Islam in chapter two, but here we give them in fuller detail in order to use them as a basis for discussing the missionary message of Islam. The five Doctrines are as follows:

1. The doctrine of Allah as the one God. This belief is interpreted to stress the unity of Allah—he can have no second —and especially is in opposition to the Christian trinitarian doctrine.[11] Allah has seven characteristics, even though his attributes cannot disclose his full nature. Allah is absolute unity and is all-seeing, all-hearing, all-speaking, all-knowing, all-willing, and all-powerful. In fact, in some ways this is the beginning and the end of all Muslim belief, for a Muslim is one who submits to the awesome, yet benevolent and merciful, fact of Allah.

2. The Angels of Allah. As with the next three doctrines, this is an adumbration on the doctrine of Allah. The Angels are the "messengers" of Allah who do his bidding to help run the universe. There is a fallen angel, Shaitan (the Hebrew Satan), who has his djinns, or spirits, as well, but all angelic beings are under Allah's control.

[11] Sura CXII is called the "unity sura" and should be referred to.

3. The Books of Allah. There are four, but each represents a portion of Allah's revelation of his eternal Book in heaven. The first three are the Torah of Moses, the Zabur or Psalms of David, and the Injul (Evangel) or Gospel of Jesus. The fourth and final Book, which supersedes all revelation in the first three, is the Qur'an.

4. The doctrine of the Prophets of Allah affirms that God has revealed his will through thousands of prophets, but especially through twenty-eight prophets, including such biblical worthies as Adam, Noah, Abraham, Elijah, John the Baptist, and Jesus. But Muhammad is represented as the final messenger and the Seal of the prophetic order.

5. The last doctrine is belief in Allah's last day, which stresses the extreme importance of Allah's final judgment and either the punishment of hell or the reward of heaven which awaits every person.

A sixth doctrine, which is not a required belief, partly because of its disputed meaning, is Kismet, fate, which is the teaching that everything which happens has been foreordained by Allah. This doctrine has led to the same sort of debate and misunderstanding as the similar Christian doctrine, but is probably best approached as another affirmation of the omniscience and omnipotence of Allah.

The Five Pillars of the Faith are duties which each Muslim must perform. They serve to remind the individual of his faith and also to bind the worldwide community of Muslims together.

1. The first duty of the Muslim is to make public confession of his faith: "There is no deity except Allah and Muhammad is the messenger of Allah." This confession is to bear witness that one is a true convert, and in the early days of Islam was a requirement for admission to the community. It is repeated frequently as an act of piety.

2. The second duty is to perform salat, or ritual prayers, five times a day. Although one performs these rituals as an individual, the fact that they are done at stated times, with all

Muslims facing Mecca, and frequently are done in concert in a mosque, enhances their unifying value for Islam.

3. Third is the duty of almsgiving. A Muslim must share his worldly goods, which Allah has given him, with those less fortunate than himself. Its obvious value as a strengthening factor in the community needs no comment.

4. Jeffery says of the fourth duty, the fast during the month of Ramadan, that "all practicing Muslims in normal health abstain from food, drink, and sexual enjoyment from the time a white thread can be distinguished from a black one in the morning till they can be no longer distinguished in the evening. At night, however, there is general rejoicing, the mosques are specially lit up for services, and there is great feasting and merriment in the houses." [12] In addition, fasting for penance and other purposes is practiced by individuals.

5. The greatest unifying duty is the pilgrimage, the *Hajj* to Mecca ("going around" the sacred places in Mecca). It is required of all Muslims, but there are reasonable exceptions and if one is unable to make the Hajj he is excused.

There is a sixth pillar of the faith, not required but implicit in the outreach of Islam. This is *Jihad*, defined by Jeffery as "Holy war, i.e., fighting against infidel peoples for the spread of Islam." [13] Since all outside the household of faith are living in *dar al harb*, the house of the enemy, it is expected that a true Muslim will devote his energies to bringing all the world under Allah's sway.

What is the record of Islam as a missionary religion through the centuries? Let us examine briefly the elements of universality, continuity, and adaptability in this religion.

The message of Islam is universal in its promises. Mankind, both male and female, is Allah's creation, and all will stand equally before his throne. Though some early Muslims of Arabian origin prided themselves upon their birthright as "close friends" or kinsmen of the Prophet, this was regarded as human vanity and not Allah's will. Islam has an enviable

[12] *Islam*, p. 192.
[13] *Ibid.*, p. 245.

record as a religion with few racial or class distinctions. Most of the Caliphs (successors) to Muhammad were sons of slave mothers, yet no stigma was attached to this fact. In contemporary Africa the Muslim appeal to Negroes is not embarrassed by any such racial discrimination as is practiced both in Christian countries and Christian communions, although it is true that Islam is concentrated almost entirely among what white Europeans call the colored races.

The Qur'an teaches that women are to be equal with men in paradise, but it also teaches that man is a grade above woman. In the words of the Qur'an: "To the faithful, both men and women, God promiseth gardens 'neath which the rivers flow, in which they shall abide, and goodly mansions in the gardens of Eden." [14] But we also read: "Men are superior to women on account of the qualities with which God hath gifted the one above the other, and on account of the outlay they make from their substance for them." [15] In orthodox practice Muslim men rule the family and wives are regarded as chattels. The wife is protected by the Qur'an, however, against divorce pronounced in anger and from many other potential abuses. The past failure of Islamic culture to give equal place to women in education, politics, and religion is being modified, but change is difficult and slow in the face of opposition by the Ulamas, the interpreters of religious law. In Turkey, for instance, the emancipation of women required the abrogation of Muslim law.

The continuity of Islam is probably stronger than either that of Buddhism or Christianity. The inclusion of large portions of Jewish and Christian scriptures as part of Allah's revelation, as well as the long line of biblical prophets who led up to Muhammad gave this religion strong traditional roots. Certain Arabic traditions, such as the sacredness of the Ka'ba, the pilgrimage to Mecca, and the belief in djinns, were taken over into the new faith as well. The person of Muhammad, the Qur'an, and, of course, the common faith

[14] Rodwell, IX:73.
[15] Ibid., IV:38.

in Allah are all important unifying factors. To these are to be added the Five Doctrines of the Creed and the Five Pillars of the Faith. The common core of Muslim faith and practice provides a powerful link between all Muslims in time and place.

It is when Islam is confronted with the task of adapting itself to new cultures and situations that most of the resistance to its missionary expansion has arisen. The Qur'an, though claimed as the actual words of Allah, definitely fits the world of its first hearers, that of seventh-century Arabia. When Islam expanded into the wider world of the Byzantine and Sassanian Empires it fell heir to these great civilizations. Islam has not continued the fantastic expansion it experienced in its first centuries, and time has proven that it is not too flexible in new situations. It has tended either to dominate and reshape the life of an area or to withdraw after initial success, and for five hundred years, until the aftermath of World War II, Islam gained almost no new territory.

One reason for this is that Islam, to be true to its nature, must require that all the world be subordinated to the will of Allah. And that will is made known specifically and finally in the Qur'an. The result of this has been to place power in the hands of the 'Ulama, the doctors of the law, those who interpret the Qur'an and know the Hadith, or Tradition. It is they who tell the community how it should be run, economically, politically, and socially. Therefore, even though there is no priestly order or class, these religious leaders have been the ruling force for centuries. As was mentioned earlier, Turkey found it necessary to break with the authority of these Ulamas to get out from under "the enormous power of tradition and the dead weight of inertia." [16]

The very meaning of Islam as submission also has serious implications for the acceptance of Western science, modern health standards, and democratic social theory by Muslims. We cite a few authorities on the ramifications of domination by the fundamentalist theology of the orthodox:

[16] Guillaume, *Islam*, p. 154.

Kenneth Cragg has said that "there is the haunting fear that family limitation may be an unwarranted interference with the Divine will—an attitude which could, of course, disqualify inoculation and even surgery in sickness and plague." [17]

Guillaume points out that no position would be open in public service if a Western-trained Muslim "expressed doubts about the Qurān being literally the word of God." [18]

Reuben Levy offers this summary:

Apart from a few small communities attracted by the teachings of some of the "reformed" sects such as those of the Bābīs, Bahā'is and adherents of the Aḥmadīya movement, Islam is at a standstill in the Western world, or is actually retreating. Political considerations apart, it would seem that the creed of Muhammad the Prophet is not suited to peoples reared in the Greek and Roman traditions and codes, which have shown themselves sufficiently elastic to permit adaptation to varying needs. As Islam stands at present, purposing to regulate and determine the minutest actions of everyday life, the faith appears on the one hand not to find approval where the individual is allowed a large measure of choice in his social conduct and of liberty in his thinking, or, on the other, where its tenets conflict with strongly held local or native tradition and doctrine.[19]

And finally, the great modern spokesman for Islam, Sir Mohammed Iqbal, has said, in a somewhat mystical vein: "For the present every Muslim nation must sink into her own deeper self, temporarily focus her vision on herself alone, until all are strong and powerful to form a living family of republics." [20]

As a missionary religion Islam's real future, like that for Buddhism and Christianity, would appear to be unpredictable.

[17] The Call of the Minaret, pp. 18-19.
[18] Islam, p. 153.
[19] The Social Structure of Islam, p. 39.
[20] Quoted in Wilfred Cantrell Smith, Islam in Modern History (Princeton: Princeton University Press, 1957), p. 82, n. 70, from The Reconstruction of Religious Thought in Islam, p. 159.

Sir Mohammed Iqbal's statement was made before the close of the colonial period which was terminated by World War II. With the rise of nationalism in Asia and Africa, Muslim countries are now able to call for religious unity in every area of national life. In the realm of science, education, and international relations this same unity could represent mono-lithic rigidity in opposition to anything modern or Western and could be a real liability to progress. But Islam has been going through the experience of coming to terms with the problem of science and religion, "biblical criticism" in relation to the Qur'an and Hadith, and the antireligious currents of secularism and nationalism, in a matter of decades, whereas Christianity has had centuries to make the same accommodation. We are much too close to these rending and shaking events in Islam to evaluate or predict their eventual results.

One surprising development, in some ways at least, is the strength of Islam's missionary expansion in sub-Saharan Africa since World War II, and the vigor of the response to its message. One hundred years ago Muslims were still actively engaged in the slave trade in this area and were not attempting to convert the natives because of the Qur'anic rule against enslaving brother Muslims. After the "Christian" countries renounced slavery and began to break up the traffic the Muslims began gradually to expand their faith into this area. Meanwhile the Protestant churches, especially under the banner of seeking to win the world for Christ in one generation, began to pour millions of dollars worth of investment into schools, hospitals, and church buildings, and to send well-trained clergymen, doctors, teachers, and social workers into Central Africa. These Christian missionaries opposed the idolatry of the natives, tried to stop polygamy, and attempted to break up many of the tribal patterns of life in the name not only of the gospel, but also of Western culture.

Meanwhile, slowly at first, but in growing numbers, and with results that have been geometric in their proportional effect, Muslim traders, merchants, and teachers and other professional persons have been spreading their faith. With little or no financial backing from a "board of missions," such a Muslim missionary might move to a Congolese village, begin to earn his living by running a store or working as a doctor, and practice his religion. Often he might marry one (or more) of the village women, and then open a small Qur'anic school to teach his children and anyone else who might be interested in learning the Qur'an and Muslim traditions. Soon he might establish a mosque—this means "standing place," and requires only a clear place of small size, with no building necessary— and begin to hold regular Friday services of prayer. He might be willing to accept—even practice—polygamy and to tolerate idolatry, at least at first. He is apt to be a colored person living the tribal ways of the people. Such missionaries appear to be far more successful in winning the people than their Christian counterparts and in terms of money spent are incomparably more efficient.

### Missionary Religions and the World Revolution

The changes that are taking place in politics, economics, and social relationships all around the world without doubt mark the times in which we live as the most revolutionary and unpredictable of all history. This is not the place to moralize about the relative potency of the three missionary religions nor to pass value judgments on them. In relation to our thesis of circles of faith it would appear, however, that their messages are not the same, either in their appeal to the needs and loyalties of men nor in their effects on the areas where they have been dominant. Each also would appear to have certain limits or flaws in its approach to potential converts. This was indicated, at least in part, in our analysis of the three elements of a missionary religion. It is also demonstrated by the fact that each has achieved only relative success, since none has ever been claimed to possess the loyalty of more than a third of the world's population.

Some real surprises have been cropping up in recent events

which indicate how easy it is to discount the inertia of great movements and how dangerous it is to underestimate the potential of the opposition. In this connection we referred briefly to the new developments in the Buddhist world where monks and nuns in Theravadin countries have taken active part in worldly politics, Christian efforts to attempt to erase some of the stigma of its record of racial intolerance and to move toward intercommunion cooperation, and the peaceful revolution in Islamic missions wherein the sword is replaced by quiet identification of the missioner with the life of his potential converts.

Now it is becoming evident that all traditional religions and religious organizations are under attack, both directly and by attrition of the prestige and power of entrenched position in political and educational leadership. The attack, which threatens all three missionary religions, comes from several directions, but especially from within each religion in the forms of nationalism and accompanying trends toward totalitarian control of a people's life, and from without in the form of secular humanisms, and especially international communism.

The Communist organizer and party worker often uses the religious convictions of his converts to ease them over to his way of thinking, but in some cases a direct attack is made on a religion. Thus in the case of Christianity it may be identified as an opiate of the people by labeling it the religion of the white races. Or the peoples of former colonial countries might be reminded of the old saying among such people: "When the white man came he had the Bible and we had the land; now we have the Bible and he has the land."

To the Buddhist, to quote from a Burmese government anti-Communist pamphlet, he will say that "Buddhism is opium of the worst kind. When the Buddha appeared 2,500 years ago, the world was in the age of slave labor. Science had not yet developed. History was not yet ripe for the concept of liberation. Therefore, the Buddha had to think up a fantastic concept of liberation—there is Nibban [nirvana] for you!" [21]

To compete with Muslim spokesmen in the Congo the Communist might remind the Congolese of the history of the slave trade, which was run largely by Arab Muslims, and state that this new interest in converting them to Islam is highly suspect.

In each case, however, the Communist is attempting to break into the circle of faith of the Christian, Buddhist, or Muslim, and he naturally attempts to find the weak places in each circle. But just because all religions are labeled by the Communist "an opiate of the masses" does not mean that men of faith need to accept this label, one which seeks to designate every religion as an enemy of mankind. Nor does it mean that in order for men of various faiths to make common cause against communism it is necessary for them to agree that all religions are the same. In fact, it would appear that the best possible defense against the blandishments of communism is for each believer to be true to his own faith.

---

[21] Dhammantarāya (Buddhism in Danger), translation of a booklet published jointly by the Ministry of Information and the Ministry of Defence, Union of Burma [1959?], p. 3.

CHAPTER 8

# JUDGE NOT, THAT
# YOU BE NOT JUDGED

Thus far we have explored seven basic areas of religious concern. In the first chapter we discussed the way in which each religion begins with certain presuppositions which the average believer takes for granted, or for which the religious teachers of that faith offer logical proof and rational explanation, but which are incapable of proof to the outsider. Thus the medieval Christian "proofs" for the existence of God are interesting exercises in logic to the nonbeliever, but if they were true proofs they should long since have brought the whole world into the circle of belief in the God of the Bible. So, too, for the belief in metempsychosis, which is basic to the faith of the Hindus, Jains, Buddhists, and Sikhs. Logical proofs for the doctrine of rebirth are available, but they tend to undergird the faith of the believer and to remain unconvincing to the outsider, unless of course he becomes persuaded—most likely for other reasons—that he really has been reborn and is in need of attaining moksha.

In chapter two we related this view concerning religious differences to the teaching about deity in various religions, taking the position that a god must be identified before he can have believers, and that the gods of various religions do not appear to be identical. The creator god of history found in the biblical story of salvation, for instance, is obviously not the same as the kami spirits of Shinto, and apparently incompatible with the Hindu teaching of the Paramatman. Chapter three examined some of the ways in which man defines the nature of his present plight, and the various sources of saving help, human and divine. The fourth area was that of the good life, the realm of ethical living, with stress on the sanctions or motivations for right thought and action. Although all religions have adherents who live by high ethical standards, the reasons for such ethical living were found to vary radically and significantly from faith to faith.

Next were explored some of the mutually exclusive claims made upon a follower of Gautama Buddha, as opposed to those made on a disciple of Confucius, Jesus Christ, or Muhammad. Chapter six dealt with some of the views of man's hopes concerning life after death. Although those beliefs about the future life chosen for consideration were markedly different one from another, each was found to be in harmony with the soteriology of the circle of faith of that religion, and to have real value for those holding such faith. Finally, an analysis of the missionary dynamics of Buddhism, Christianity, and Islam disclosed striking variations in such vital areas as the universality of the message of each religion and of its relevance to society and history. It is to be hoped that these chapters have demonstrated the validity of the claim that the differences between the religions of mankind are significant and must be dealt with in any approach to understand the faiths of other men.

As has been indicated, this is not to ignore the large areas of agreement between any two religions, nor those to be found among all religions, but it is to take the unpopular position of opposing those who continue to insist that all religions are simply different roads to a common goal. With goals differing as widely as "extinction of self" and "the kingdom of

God," it must matter greatly which religion a person follows. Or rather, if a person is trying to arrive at a proper understanding of his own religion in relation to that of another, it is no help to have exponents of "the unity of all religions" insisting that it does not matter to which religion one belongs. For if it does not matter, then Adolf Hitler was as right as Moses, or Jesus Christ. If it makes no difference, all the sacrifices of the martyrs, or the agony of the Jews at Buchenwald, are made a mockery, and the cynical remark of Koheleth applies. "For the fate of the sons of men and the fate of the beasts is the same; as one dies, so dies the other. They all have the same breath, and man has no advantage over the beasts; for all is vanity." [1]

It is true that there are persons who are convinced that religion is of the utmost importance, but who also believe that there are no basic or significant differences between religions. It would appear, however, that this point of view is exactly that, a point of view which is one of the several basic possibilities among the religions. Thus Aldous Huxley's position, as expressed in *The Perennial Philosophy*, owed much to Hindu Vedanta, as he was quite willing to concede. The only consideration to stress here is that when someone insists on the basic unity of all religions, he is doing so in the context of his circle of faith, the circle of faith which starts with the assumption that there is, for instance, a ground of being which is the source of all creation, and the fountainhead of all religions. But he is not making an objective or demonstrable statement which will commend itself as true to all who are willing to examine it with an open mind.

### Some Prerequisites for Dialogue Between Men of Different Faiths

Although the fields of cultural anthropology and social psychology are young, they have contributed a great deal to our understanding of man as a social being, especially in the

[1] Eccl. 3:19.

problem of communication and dialogue between persons with differing backgrounds. During World War II the War Information Office commissioned a study of Japanese culture which was of great value in the conduct of the war with Japan and to the government of occupation. The study, remarkable because the author was unable to visit Japan, is an introduction to the psychology of the Japanese and their social manners and customs which can illustrate to Americans how differently another culture can view the meaning of life and the nature of society.

*The Silent Language* by Edward Hall is an analysis of the unspoken language which every culture develops, which tends to be a barrier to understanding between different cultures. In the chapter "Space Speaks" he illustrates the differences in the way spatial distance is used as an unspoken language.

In Latin America the interaction distance is much less than it is in the United States. Indeed, people cannot talk comfortably with one another unless they are very close to the distance that evokes either sexual or hostile feelings in the North American. The result is that when they move close, we withdraw and back away. As a consequence, they think we are distant or cold, withdrawn and unfriendly. We, on the other hand, are constantly accusing them of breathing down our necks, crowding us, and spraying our faces.[2]

This illustration might help us understand better the word of Jesus quoted as the title of this chapter, "Judge not, that you be not judged." [3] This phrase is often misquoted by using only the first two words, "Judge not," to imply that one should never judge another person. This is patently not its real meaning, for of course we do judge others all the time, whether it is in choosing a companion for a walk down the street, a husband or wife as a lifetime companion, or a candidate for a term of office. But if we are aware that our judgments are but extensions of our limited human understanding and prejudices, and that our fellow man is judging us in the same

---

[2] (New York: Doubleday & Company, 1959).
[3] Matt. 7:1.

manner, perhaps we might be able to judge with more charity and tolerance and with less dogmatic conviction that we are right and the other fellow is wrong. This sort of tolerance, however, might require a new approach to theological discussion, at least as it usually is engaged in. Most discussion among Christians, for instance, falls into two categories, polemics and apologetics. Unfortunately, neither the language of polemics nor apologetics is appropriate for a discussion among men of different faiths. From early Christian times the term "dialogue" has been used to describe such a conversation, however, and recently it is being used more and more. For instance, Hendrik Kraemer has entitled a book *World Cultures and World Religions: the Coming Dialogue*,[4] while Professor Ninian Smart has actually written a volume called *A Dialogue of Religions*,[5] which consists of an imaginary dialogue between a Christian, a Jew, a Muslim, a Hindu, a Buddhist from Ceylon, and one from Japan.

If one desires to move away from the apologetic position which so easily leads to the charge of intolerance and chooses instead to attempt to involve himself and others in genuine dialogue about the meaning of the circles of faith which we have been describing, one other thing needs to be stressed. Instead of searching for truth and for proof of the rightness of one's own convictions, one must remember that a dialogue is between two persons and is neither a monologue nor a sermon preached to bring the other person under conviction of the truth as you see it. It must be a dialogue in which one person shares the meaning of his faith with another person rather than seeks to communicate knowledge, and where one remembers that he is describing commitment to his own faith rather than attempting to use reason to convince the other to change his mind. In other words, the purpose is that of mutual understanding rather than the desire to offer proofs of truth. But above all it must be remembered that a dialogue means that the other person must be listened to and responded

[4] (Philadelphia: The Westminster Press, 1961).
[5] (Naperville, Ill.: Alec R. Allenson, 1960).

to, that his integrity must be respected just as you want your own to be respected.

## Circles of Faith Among Biblical Religions

The chart shown on the next page diagrams the relationship between three of the four biblical religions, all of which fit into a larger circle of monotheistic faith. Zoroastrianism has been omitted only for brevity, although its omission in no way affects the meaning of the diagram, and it properly belongs in this grouping. At the center where all three circles overlap is an area which represents man as mankind in search of meaning for his life. This is to assume that all men are essentially equal, with the same human passions, needs, hopes, and fears. But in this diagram each man is also represented as either a Jew, a Christian, or a Muslim, and would be at home only in the main area of one of the three overlapping circles.

The great circle which surrounds the three is intended to represent a conviction common to the three religions, belief in a creator God who has made the world and man, who has an overarching purpose for all mankind, who reveals his purpose to man through prophets (spokesmen), and whose revelation has been preserved in sacred writings, the scriptures of the three faiths. Whether or not the deities of the three religions, Yahweh for Judaism, "the God and father of our Lord Jesus Christ" for the Christian, and Allah for the Muslim, are one and the same is not capable of demonstration, and it appears obvious that there is a long history of failure on the part of theologians among these religions to arrive at agreement on this question. Yet the use of a single large circle to represent this monotheistic premise appears to be justified and in itself not to be particularly controversial.

When we look at the three small areas where any two of the circles overlap we find represented areas of common agreement between the two circles of faith. Thus both Judaism and Islam accept the Torah of Moses and the Psalms of David as true revelation, the Jews and the Christians have in com-

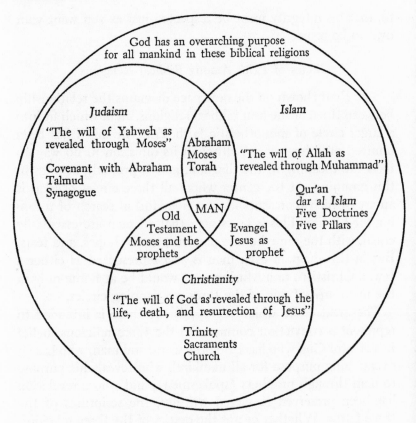

God has an overarching purpose
for all mankind in these biblical religions

*Judaism*

"The will of Yahweh as
revealed through Moses"

Covenant with Abraham
Talmud
Synagogue

Abraham
Moses
Torah

*Islam*

"The will of Allah as
revealed through Muhammad"

Qur'an
dar al *Islam*
Five Doctrines
Five Pillars

Old
Testament
Moses and the
prophets

MAN

Evangel
Jesus as
prophet

*Christianity*

"The will of God as revealed through the
life, death, and resurrection of Jesus"

Trinity
Sacraments
Church

BIBLICAL CIRCLES OF FAITH

mon the Old Testament, while Muslims and Christians share
the Injul (Evangel) of Jesus, and the Muslims revere many
of the early Christian leaders (including Jesus) as prophets.

The large area in each circle represents that which is unique,
or special to that religion. This has to do with two things—
the nature of the revelation given by God, and the nature of
the community, with its traditions, which forms the religion.
Thus for Judaism the will of its God was revealed through
Moses, and membership in the circle of Jewish faith includes

210

acceptance of God's covenant with Abraham, the truth of the Talmud as definitive for the meaning and application of the Law of Moses, and membership in the synagogue for those in the true community. For Christianity the final revelation of God's purpose was through Jesus Christ, and most Christians have as common denominators belief in the Trinity, the use of the sacraments, and fellowship in the church. The Muslim believes that the final revelation of the will of Allah was through his messenger, Muhammad, and holds in common with other Muslims the Qur'an as revealed truth, dar al Islam as the brotherhood of true Muslims, and the Five Doctrines and the Five Pillars of the Faith as basic to his life.

The above description is almost trite in that it simply lists what members of each of these faiths hold in common, but if we think in terms of the differences between any two circles of faith it might help us see the problems involved when men of different faiths attempt to arrive at understanding and agreement. We already have pointed out that the basic difference between Jew, Christian, and Muslim lies in the understanding each has concerning the nature and vehicle of God's revelation—whether it was through Moses and the Torah, Jesus and the New Testament, or Muhammad and the Qur'an. But a further cause of friction is due to the fact that both the Christian and Muslim scriptures contain passages which condemn the Jews for their lack of true faith—their failure to accept the later revelations as true—while the Qur'an contains both anti-Jewish and anti-Christian passages. What is probably the earliest Christian writing to be preserved, Paul's First Letter to the Thessalonians, contains this charge against the Jews, which, although it was obviously not what would be called today "anti-Semitic," nevertheless has been interpreted, along with other New Testament passages, by many Christians as justifying anti-Semitism.

For you, brethren, became imitators of the churches of God in Christ Jesus which are in Judea; for you suffered the same things from your own countrymen as they did from the Jews, who killed both the Lord Jesus and the prophets, and drove us out, and displease God and oppose all men by hindering us from speaking to the Gentiles that they may be saved—so as always to fill up the measure of their sins. But God's wrath has come upon them at last! [6]

The Qur'an, which is ambivalent toward the Jews and Christians, also, at times, has strong words of condemnation for both. Thus in Sura V, "The Table Spread," we read:

O Believers! take not the Jews or Christians as friends. They are but one another's friends. If any one of you taketh them for his friends, he surely is one of them! God will not guide the evil doers. [And again:] Infidels now are they who say, "God (Allah) is the Messiah, Son of Mary"; for the Messiah said, "O children of Israel! worship God, my Lord and your Lord." Whoever shall join other gods with God, God shall forbid him the Garden, and his abode shall be the Fire; and the wicked shall have no helpers. [7]

And finally, a verse which condemns the Jews but praises some Christians: "Of all men thou wilt certainly find the Jews, and those who join other gods with God [Allah], to be the most intense in hatred of those who believe; and thou shalt certainly find those to be nearest to them in affection who say, 'We are Christians.' This, because some of them are priests and monks, and because they are free from pride." [8]

The history of the biblical religions is one of almost unbelievable animosity, butchery, and constant warfare. [9] The anti-Semitism of the Christians, the Crusades of the Christians against the Muslims, and the centuries of Muslim Jihad where entire nations were arrayed in holy war against "unbelievers," make disturbing reading for one interested in working toward world brotherhood and agreement among members of different

[6] I Thess. 2:14-16.
[7] Rodwell, vss. 56, 76.
[8] Ibid., vs. 85.
[9] Although in the Christian era the Jews have received most of the persecution from Christians and Muslims, in the Old Testament books of history there is frequent reference to waging "holy war" at the command of Yahweh.

religions. But today if one were to say that the problem of the Arab-Israeli conflict could be settled if only the Jews were to accept Muhammad as the true Prophet, or the Muslims were to renounce Muhammad and agree to follow the Law of Moses, who would there be to listen to him? And Christians have tried, often in the most peaceful manner, for almost two thousand years to convince the Jews that Jesus really was the long-promised Jewish Messiah, with but meager results. And as was noted in the chapter on missionary religions, Muslims have had far better success in converting Christians than have Christians in converting Muslims.

This story of intolerance among members of biblical faiths is known across the world, and the resentment felt by Hindus, Buddhists, Confucianists, and persons of other faiths who have been the target for conversion, especially by the Christian and Muslim, is far deeper and more widespread than most Christian missionaries, for instance, are willing to admit. A most interesting essay by B. W. Williams, called *The Joke of Christianizing China*, appeared in 1927, and it argues most cogently that the Christians should never have tried to Christianize China, that they have no real hope of succeeding, and that the meager results, in terms of the money and manpower spent, are scandalous. He concludes his essay, written more than twenty years before the Communist regime took over, with this paragraph, in the pamphleteering style of a religious tract:

The Chinese have as much right to conduct their civil and religious institutions according to their own notions as we have to follow our preferences. There would be no more impropriety in their attempting to Confucianize our country than there is in our effort to Christianize theirs. Why can't Western nations attend to their own business and let China do as she pleases with her own? Hands off. Quit meddling. Use horse sense. Let China be for the Chinese.[10]

[10] (New York: Peter Eckler Publishing Company, 1927).

Others have raised their voices in protest against what they call the intolerance and arrogance of biblical religions. One is Arnold J. Toynbee, who takes the position in a monograph on *Christianity Among the Religions of the World*,[11] that the great monotheistic faiths, Judaism, Christianity, and Islam, have been, and continue to be, guilty of gross intolerance. By their claims to possess exclusive truth they have fostered war and division in a world which desires peace and reconciliation. At the same time he praises Hinduism and Buddhism for their tolerance and their long history of relatively peaceful and nonproselytizing activity.

### Circles of Faith Among the World's Religions

With these charges against the biblical faiths before us, let us first describe a second chart which diagrams all of the major religions in terms of circles of faith, and then in terms of these basic patterns let us examine the question of whether intolerance is endemic only among biblical faiths, or whether it is not actually a characteristic of each religion. In this chart we again have three circles, although there is no large circle around the entire diagram. If such an all-encompassing circle were used it would have to be drawn by a member of one faith who was attempting to include all religions under the aegis of his own faith. Thus a Christian might draw such an inclusive circle and label it "The Creator God of the Bible and his plan of salvation for the entire world." A Hindu might label such a circle "The all-encompassing World-soul from which and to which is all existence." And a Taoist might use the label "The mystical Tao which, although unnamed, informs all things and makes existence possible."

Since we have already discussed the biblical circle (except for Zoroastrianism), let us look first at the circle containing the four religions which stem from India. These are Hinduism, Jainism, Buddhism, and the religion of the Sikhs. Each of these holds in common a doctrine of rebirth, the concept of

[11] (New York: Charles Scribner's Sons, 1957).

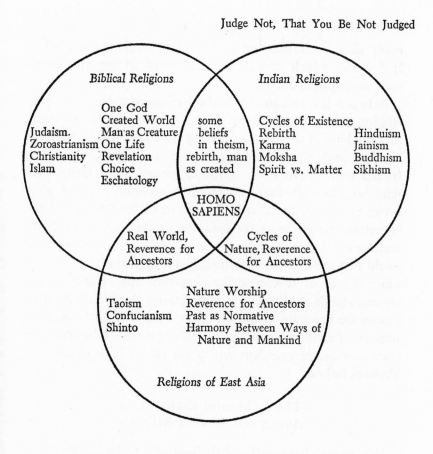

**Biblical Religions**

Judaism.
Zoroastrianism
Christianity
Islam

One God
Created World
Man as Creature
One Life
Revelation
Choice
Eschatology

some
beliefs
in theism,
rebirth, man
as created

HOMO
SAPIENS

**Indian Religions**

Cycles of Existence
Rebirth               Hinduism
Karma                 Jainism
Moksha                Buddhism
Spirit vs. Matter     Sikhism

Real World,
Reverence for
Ancestors

Cycles of
Nature, Reverence
for Ancestors

Taoism
Confucianism
Shinto

Nature Worship
Reverence for Ancestors
Past as Normative
Harmony Between Ways of
Nature and Mankind

**Religions of East Asia**

CIRCLES OF FAITH

cycles of existence, karma (although interpreted differently by
each religion), and moksha (release) as the goal of spiritual
striving, while each has a tendency to regard spirit as good,
and matter as evil, or at least as an encumbrance to spirit. For
East Asia we find Taoism, Confucianism, and Shinto as shar-
ing concern for some kind of nature worship, a reverence for
ancestors (or at least for the way of idealized ancients), for
regarding an idealized past as normative, and as seeking the
goal of harmony between the ways of nature and mankind. As
was shown for the biblical religions in the first diagram, within
both the Indian and the East Asian circles of faith there exist

215

many differences between each of the religions included in that circle, which could be diagrammed in separate charts with overlapping circles.

Between the Indian and biblical religions there is an overlapping area of common, or similar, belief, such as the belief in some kind of theism, e.g., among the Sikhs, or among some Hindus, and, outside India, among some Buddhists. The Indian faiths have some common ground with East Asian religions, especially in Taoist monistic thought, or concern for cycles of nature, and also in the reverence for the way of the ancestors. There is also the common ground between biblical and East Asian religions in an emphasis on this present real world of time and space (which is not typical of India), and some degree of reverence for ancestors. And finally, *homo sapiens* stands at the center, representing the fact that all religions are made up of the beliefs and practices of human beings, and that all religions partake of our common humanity in their mixture of grandeur and pettiness, of high claims and abysmal failures.

### The Problem of Exclusiveness Among the World's Religions

We already have outlined the sort of intolerance displayed by the biblical religions, and although we will come back to a discussion of the meaning of this intolerance we now will discuss the problem of exclusiveness in the message of salvation of other world religions. This will provide a basis for viewing biblical intolerance from a little different perspective. It is customary to accuse biblical religions of intolerance because of teachings such as this found in the New Testament book of Acts, where we read, in reference to Jesus Christ, "there is salvation in no one else, for there is no other name under heaven given among men by which we must be saved." [12] But when we turn to the religions in the Indian and East Asian

[11] Acts 4:12.

circles of faith, we find that each of them also contains teachings which exclude from salvation certain classes or groups
of persons, at least insofar as this present existence is concerned. In fact, the question should be raised in this connection, if everybody has available whatever saving help he needs
during this life and will reach a positive destiny at death, why
would a religion have a message of salvation in the first place?
Let us look briefly at some illustrations of this phenomenon
of exclusiveness among representative religions.

*Hinduism.* Shortly after the United States Supreme Court
1954 ruling which outlawed segregation in the public schools
*The New Yorker* carried a cartoon showing two Hindus reading an American newspaper. The caption read: "What are
these Americans so upset about? You'd think they had to
live with untouchables!" It is true that India is a land that
prides itself as one that possesses a high measure of spirituality,
but it also has a record of rigid class distinction supported by
strong religious sanctions.

Of the three main ways to salvation in Hinduism the way
of works, Karma-marga, is the most exclusive. Sometimes
called Brahmanism, this way adheres to the teachings of the
Laws of Manu concerning birth, i.e., class, or caste. The highest three, or twice-born, classes, the Brahman, Kshatriya, and
Vaishya, are considered to be spiritually superior to the Sudras
(blacks) and outcastes. And only the Brahman can hope for
nirvana, or union of his atman with the paramatman at death,
while his wife probably must be reborn at least one more time.
Many religious privileges such as temple worship were in the
recent past actually forbidden to the person of low birth and
to the outcaste.

The second way of salvation is the path of knowledge. It is
by definition restricted to the few who have the time, inclina-
tion, and perseverance to achieve yoga, or union with god, in
this way. And the yogi who achieves status as a religious guide
is held to be superior to the ordinary run of men. Salvation,
though in theory open to many, is in practice attained by
very few.

Even bhakti-marga, the path of devotion to the god, Vishnu, or of Shiva, has not been available to all. First, the outcastes have been excluded from temple and festival rites—even after federal law opened the temples during the early days of the Republic of India this segregation persisted. Again, the followers of Shiva often scorn those of Vishnu, and the reverse is also true, although for the most part there is little friction between these major sects, and it is even possible to follow both at the same time. The teachings of the Laws of Manu also tend to offset even the implied universalism of bhakti-marga. For even though the way of devotion is supposed to be open to anyone, the teaching that those who are born into a lower caste are working out a just punishment for sins in a former life tends to override the help promised by devotion to a god.

A final consideration is the fact that it is not possible for one who is not born a Hindu to enter into its system of salvation. Class or birth is normative, and if you are not born into an actual caste you are non-Hindu. In spite of the obvious pride with which the English regarded themselves while they were the rulers of India, they were simply beef-eating scum from the point of view of upper-caste Hindus. Gandhi, for instance, as well as his whole family, had to purify himself from the defilement of leaving the sacred land of India and for the time he spent living in England.

Jainism. Before discussing who can be saved according to the teachings of Buddhism a brief comment is in order concerning its twin religion, Jainism. This religion probably is the most exclusive of all in its requirements for salvation. Each person must save himself by the practice of extreme asceticism or self-discipline. This is necessary in order to sever all possible attachments to the world and to avoid all actions or thoughts which might add to the load of karma which holds one's jiva, or soul, in captivity to this evil world. But this is not all. Very few are able to embark on this extreme venture to seize nirvana or moksha by main strength, as it were. More than that, it is also Jain teaching that in this present, decadent

218

period of history no one at all is able to reach final moksha, or release. Instead, all souls in bondage must wait for a new age to come, thousands of years from now.[13]

*Buddhism.* One of the most interesting limitations on the teaching of universal salvation in Buddhism concerns the problem of birth. Although Gautama was of the Kshatriya class and taught that salvation was not restricted to the Brahman, or priest, from earliest times certain qualifications seem to have been prerequisite to the attainment of Buddahood. It is taught that Gautama, the historical Buddha, had perfected himself through many existences as a god and as a man. At last he was deserving of the final achievement of Enlightenment. As was pointed out earlier, even a god must be reborn in this world, as a human male, before he is eligible for final nirvana. Thus women are considered dubious prospects for the achievement of passionless peace, although some are believed to have made the grade. But the vast mass of the Buddhist laity in Theravadin (Hinayana) countries of Southern Asia are assumed to be doomed to further rebirths. In other words, one must not only renounce the world but also begin to predicate his hope for salvation on being a human male, with the assumption that he has a long string of excellent lives behind him.

In Mahayana Buddhism the situation would appear to be not too different from the attitude in Christianity. Salvation is for those who trust in Bodhisattvas, and who fulfill the various requirements of the religion. The rest are doomed to hells and to rebirth. But even sectarian jealousy raises its ugly head. E. L. Allen, for instance, pointed out that "in Japan, Nichiren [founder of Amida] did not doubt that all forms of Buddhism save his own were pernicious." [14]

*East Asian religions.* Since the religions of China and Japan usually are thought of as less aggressive than those of India or the biblical lands, let us make brief mention of the ways in

[13] Basham, *The Wonder That Was India*, p. 290.
[14] "The Christian Attitude Toward the Non-Christian Religions," *The Journal of Religious Thought*, XII, (Autumn-Winter, 1954-55), 20.

which salvation is limited, thereby made exclusive, in East Asia. In the monistic philosophy known as Taoism, all existence is explained in terms of the various ways in which the underlying force of nature, the Tao, gives expression to itself. In this present life only a few are expected to learn the secret of Tao and thus be able to live by it, or to become a man of Tao. Man's plight is caused by ignorance of Tao, by trying to change the natural order of the universe by human striving and meddling. The following description of the "unsaved man" is given in the Tao Tê Ching:

> "He who stands on tip-toe, does not stand firm;
> He who takes the longest strides, does not walk the fastest."
> He who does his own looking sees little,
> He who defines himself is not therefore distinct.
> He who boasts of what he will do succeeds in nothing;
> He who is proud of his work, achieves nothing that endures.[15]

This is the way of most men, including the Confucian Sage who was condemned by the Taoists because of his stress upon education in order to impose on man artificial rules which would inhibit his natural instincts. By contrast the saved man, the man of peace, contentment, and possessed of real and effective power, is the man who knows the way of Tao and goes along with it.

> Of old those that were the best officers of Court
> Had inner natures subtle, abstruce, mysterious, penetrating,
> Too deep to be understood.[16]

On the other hand the rival Confucianists had their own teachings which were exclusive in nature. As was pointed out in chapters four and five, the teachings of Confucius are predicated upon a feudal system with a ranking of superior and inferior persons, and also upon the ideal of the chün tzu. This

---

[15] Waley, The Way and Its Power, XXIV:1-6.
[16] Ibid., XV:1-3.

was the scholarly gentleman who achieved true nobility by his Confucian learning and by practicing the ancient feudal virtues. By definition only the scholar can become a chün tzu, and some groups, such as the soldier and merchant, are placed low in the scale of human values because they are far removed from the ideal. This ideal was also not expected to be attained by mere females. Finally, the true ancestor is one who has sons to carry on his name and to revere it in future generations. The man without sons is a man who has lost his salvation.

It is not enough, however, merely to quote the Tao Tê Ching and to refer to Confucian ideals in order to document the claim that intolerance is found throughout India and East Asia. It also is necessary to emphasize that the notion that the East is spiritual, otherworldly, and peaceful, while the West is materialistic, worldly, and warlike, simply does not fit the facts of history. The recent partition of British India into Pakistan and Hindustan, for instance, was attended by some of the most violent intercommunal religious rioting of all time. In China, for many centuries, Buddhism and Taoism were deadly enemies, the fortunes of each being determined to a large degree by which religion was favored by the ruling house. Richard H. Robinson says that there were famous Buddhist teachers in the sixth century in China on whom royal favor was lavished. "The one exception to this royal favour was a brief period of proscription in North China about A.D. 575, when three hundred thousand monks and nuns were forcibly returned to secular life." [17] Again, in connection with a discussion of the arrival in China of Buddhism "with a world-view and a set of institutions that were incompatible with many parts of the native culture," he says that although Buddhism demanded exclusive allegiance, it did not enforce it, "with the result that it did not obliterate its rivals.

"Buddhism's chief rival was organized Taoism. The two religions are similar in some ways. . . . In spite of extensive

[17] "Buddhism: in China and Japan," in Zaehner, The Concise Encyclopedia of Living Faiths, p. 323.

mutual influence the two religions are incompatible and have
remained in opposition throughout the ages." [18]

There is need only to refer to the basis in Shinto for the
World War II policy of the Japanese to bring all the surrounding countries into the orbit of the Greater East-Asia Co-
prosperity Sphere, a messianic desire on the part of the
Japanese nation which was not shared by their neighbors.

If we agree that each of the religions of the world has its
own version of exclusiveness in describing who is saved and
who is not, how is one to account for the more violent forms
of missionary zeal to be found, especially among biblical religions? It would appear that the significant difference in the
sense of urgency between religions following the basic biblical
perspective and that, for instance, following the Indian perspective is to be found in the factor of time. A man marooned
on a tropical island has no concern for such considerations as
TV schedules, voting days, doctors' hours, or payday. A New
Yorker, on the other hand, must have a real sense of time and
of its daily fluctuations, or he will feel lost and bewildered as
life goes rushing by him.

Biblical religions are unique in their view of man, of the
world, and of history in the stress placed upon the choice
every man must make. Christianity, for instance, teaches that
each person is a unique creation who lives but one life. In this
one life he is confronted with the choice between good and
evil, between serving God or the devil, choosing between life
and death. But man has only this one chance—not many
chances, as in Hinduism—so that the choice is both poignant
and final. Therefore the Christian missionary has a tremendous
concern that all men know of this choice and make the right
one. Christian and Muslim eschatologies stress the ultimate
nature of this decision by emphasizing the rewards and punishments of heaven and hell. Note the urgency in such New
Testament passages as the following: "Truly, I say to you, you
will not have gone through all the towns of Israel, before the

[18] *Ibid.*, pp. 333-34.

Son of man comes." [19] In his letter to the Romans, Paul quotes the prophet Joel: "Every one who calls upon the name of the Lord will be saved." And then he adds: "But how are men to call upon him in whom they have not believed? And how are they to believe in him of whom they have never heard? And how are they to hear without a preacher? And how can men preach unless they are sent? As it is written, 'How beautiful are the feet of those who preach good news!' " [20]

There is no comparable sense of urgency to be found in Hinduism or Buddhism because the view of man and of history is of another kind. By comparison the Indian view appears to be tolerant and relaxed. But if the Hindu or Buddhist accuses the Christian or Muslim of intolerance and arrogance, is it not possible also, although in caricature, to depict the Indian position as one of spiritual arrogance and in the last analysis of intolerance? The Hindu or Buddhist, for instance, says in effect: "You poor Christian. You came to us all excited about your little portion of truth. You are just like a little child who finds a bit of broken mirror and thinks the glittering object is the sun itself. But we will not worry about you. You will have many, many more lives in which to discover the truth taught by the Buddha. We are willing to welcome you, even in this present life, as a fellow traveler along the path to final nirvana. But since we believe that ultimately every blade of grass and every sentient being will achieve nirvana, we will not urge or push you into the true way. In time after many redeaths and rebirths you finally will come to know what we already know."

### The Gospel and Other Faiths

It obviously is important to try to understand the beliefs and point of view of the other person, but it also is necessary to be aware of the limitations to this understanding. One thing

[19] Matt. 10:23.
[20] Rom. 10:13-15.

223

to be wary of is the assumption that if only persons knew each other better there would be no problems or friction between persons or groups. Yet we are reminded that the countries which shared the highest percentage of exchange students between them between the two world wars were France and Germany. Again, the KKK members of the deep South know their Negro neighbors better than a Yankee New Englander ever could. And a husband or wife might know the relatives of his spouse very well and be very sorry for that fact.

It should be obvious from all that has been said that I think that the idea of a world faith for all men is not a logical possibility. But just because a synthetic world faith cannot be devised to snare the loyalty of all men does not validate the position that "What one believes really does not matter." If an understanding of one's life "makes no difference," then life has no meaning. But if one is responsible and seeks to discover what life is all about, there also are no short cuts. Quite often a person begins the study of world religions with the assumption, tacit or expressed, that if he studies all the religions he will find the one that suits him best. But this, too, is impossible. One cannot really understand a religion other than his own unless he first enters into that circle of faith with real sympathy—and then he has relinquished his assumed objectivity about the faith. It is not possible, in other words, to try out all religions as one might sample a tray of hors d'oeuvres. To become such a human chameleon would be to lose all critical ability, even if it were possible to stand within more than one circle of faith at the same time.

How then should a Christian approach a study of other religions? How can he talk with a Hindu or a Buddhist so as to share his thoughts and concerns about religion and his understanding of life with the non-Christian? How can he in turn learn from the man of another faith, and yet not be guilty of feelings of superiority or condescension, or of feeling threatened by the other person's faith?

The first task that the Christian faces is to learn the difference between the gospel and the particular form of Christianity which he represents. Even though the human tendency to equate one's understanding of the gospel with the real thing is as old as Christianity itself, nevertheless it remains a problem. Hendrik Kraemer's position is valid that Christianity must always be regarded by the Christian as a religion among other religions, even though it claims to possess the gospel of God. Within twenty years after the death of Jesus we find Paul intensely concerned with this problem. He wrote to the Galatians in very strong language to turn back to the true gospel:

I am astonished that you are so quickly deserting him who called you in the grace of Christ and turning to a different gospel— not that there is another gospel, but there are some who trouble you and want to pervert the gospel of Christ. But even if we, or an angel from heaven, should preach to you a gospel contrary to that which we preached to you, let him be accursed. As we have said before, so now I say again, If any one is preaching to you a gospel contrary to that which you received, let him be accursed.[21]

Again and again in his letters Paul attacks the members of the various churches because they attempt to live by man's ways rather than to follow the gospel. At Corinth he opposed the formation of factions whose members were following Peter, or Apollos, or Paul. To the Thessalonians he wrote concerning problems of thought and practice which were dividing the community or causing confusion and worry. And to all of the churches he wrote expressing concern that, though they possessed the good news of God's salvation offered by faith in Christ, they do not live by that gospel. The Corinthians fought among themselves just as fiercely as many modern congregations. All forms of Christianity, whether Roman Catholic, Quaker, Methodist, Eastern Orthodox, or Syrian, come under the judgment of the gospel as human organizations with human limitations.

For this reason the Christian has no choice but to bow in

[21] Gal 1:6-8.

225

humility when a Hindu points out that Christians are guilty of adultery, drunkenness, murder, envy, jealousy, racial discrimination, witch burning, "holy" crusades, church politics, the Ku Klux Klan, and every conceivable form of corruption and evil-doing. But the Christian need not agree with the conclusion that this fact of Christian shortcomings either invalidates the gospel or that it is a true expression of the gospel. Every human expression of religion is prone to the selfish and cruel interests of individuals. When Katherine Mayo wrote *Mother India* she was accused of falsifying the record, of giving a completely unfair picture of Indian life and of having no understanding of true Hinduism. Yet most of her descriptions and charges undoubtedly were true or had solid basis in fact. But they were not true of the best that Hinduism or Hindus had to offer, nor was her interpretation the only valid one.

The Christian gospel remains the gospel of God only when it is proclaimed freely as a judgment upon all man's endeavors to run his own life or to claim to know the mind of God. Every Christian and every form of Christianity stands as much under the judgment of the gospel as does the non-Christian and all non-Christian religions. A missionary who goes to India to proclaim the gospel, therefore, should expect to find himself judged by the very standards he preaches. In the words of Paul: "Therefore you have no excuse, O man, whoever you are, when you judge another; for in passing judgment upon him you condemn yourself, because you, the judge, are doing the very same things." [22] And he should not be surprised at critical questions about the divisiveness of Christianity and about the fact that most of the great wars of modern times have been between Christian nations.

What then is a possible basis for dialogue between the Christian and the non-Christian? In a lecture, *The Gospel, Christianity, and Other Faiths*, Heinrich Frick suggested that one way of expressing this problem is by imagining a triangle.[23]

[22] Rom. 2:1.
[23] Tr. by James Haire (Oxford: Basil Blackwell & Mott, 1938), p. 46.

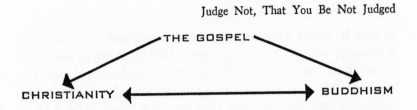

THE GOSPEL

CHRISTIANITY ←――――――――――――→ BUDDHISM

At the apex should be placed the gospel. At the left-hand base corner is to be placed Christianity and at the right-hand base corner "other faiths," or perhaps a single faith, such as Buddhism. In this diagram, which admittedly is an attempt to present the Christian understanding of the problem, the Christian and, in this case, the Buddhist stand face to face. Each is a man in history surrounded by all the limitations of his humanity. Each can communicate with the other as a man seeking to understand his own life and seeking to share with the other his fears, hopes, and insights. When the Christian tells the Buddhist of his Christian gospel, he does so not as one who possesses it as his own truth but as one who is witnessing to its truth and its claims upon him. He is willing to submit to the judgment which this gospel brings upon his own life and the life of his church. But he also seeks to communicate to the Buddhist the meaning and the help which this gospel has given to his life. To the Buddhist who is under the conviction that to live is to suffer he offers the promise of meaning and hope as found by faith in Christ, the message that there is a God who cares.

For his part, the Buddhist does not start with the position that there is a God who has spoken in terms of the gospel message. But as a man caught in the despair of existence he is interested in learning what the Christian has found to be of help. He also is eager to tell the Christian of the Four Noble Truths and of his conviction that the Lord Buddha has taught the Way to cessation of suffering. If each is sincere, the problem of whether either is able completely to live up to the ideal of his religion should not be at issue. Instead, each would be seeking both to share his most valuable possession and also to listen to the other's message. And if the Christian

227

is able to listen with an open heart he cannot help but hear a message which has brought hope and meaning to hundreds of millions. And to hear this message should make him less sure that his own understanding of the gospel is the only possible one and also less sure that everyone must believe as he does.

But there is something even more important which such an encounter might accomplish. If every Christian were made responsible for the understanding of his own faith in such a way that he could explain it clearly to others, much would be gained. For until one understands his own faith he has no right to claim it to be true. And if he truly understands it he will be much less sure that his own understanding of it is the last word, or even that Christianity is the sole possessor of salvation. When Jesus said, "Judge not, that you be not judged," he also added, "For with the judgment you pronounce you will be judged." Or as Rabbi Hillel said some years before Jesus, "Judge not thy fellow until thou art come to his place, and say not of a thing which cannot be understood that it will be understood in the end." [24]

The subtitle of this book is "A Preface to the Study of the World's Religions," and it is intended to be just that. The future of religious thought undoubtedly will have a large place in it for discussions of the nature and meaning of the faiths of other men, and it is to be hoped that this volume will lead the reader to study further in the fascinating area of world religions. It might be most fitting to close with a quotation from an outstanding Roman Catholic scholar in this field, R. C. Zaehner, who in turn quotes an eminent Protestant scholar in the camp of the radical biblicism of the neo-orthodox movement:

One thing . . . seems certain, and that is that the differences that separate the great religions will not, in the foreseeable future, suddenly evaporate into any "higher synthesis," but will

[24] Herbert Danby, tr., *The Mishnah* (New York: Oxford University Press, 1933), Nezikin: Aboth 2:5, p. 448.

continue to preach their different messages, seeking to save and comfort souls according to what they believe to be the truth; "for what is needed in the present time of world-encounter of religions," as Hendrik Kraemer rightly says, "is not to be as sweet as possible with each other, but to learn the art of being as true as possible with each other, in spiritual emulation." [25]

[25] *The Concise Encyclopedia of Living Faiths*, p. 417, and quoting Hendrik Kraemer, *Religion and the Christian Faith* (London: Lutterworth Press, 1956), p. 134.

# BIBLICAL INDEX

231

# GENERAL INDEX

233

Confucius—cont'd
  human destiny, 149
  life and teachings, 124-31
  name and dates, 24
Cragg, Kenneth, 193n., 199
Cranston, Ruth, 12n.
Creel, H. G., 127, 129

"D" source, 96
Dar al harb, 196
Dar al Islam, 211
Das, Bhagavan, 13n.
Dead Sea Scrolls, 116
Decalogues, 96-97
Declaration of Independence, 29
Deity
  biblical teaching, 34-39
  Buddhist teachings, 44-47
  Confucian teaching, 51-52
  Hindu teachings, 41-43
  Islamic teaching, 39-40
  in world's religions, 53-56
  Jain teachings, 43-44
  Shinto teaching, 52
Demythologize, 146
Dhammapada, 104-5
Dharma, 158
Diagram
  Christian-Buddhist, 227
  Confucian relationships, 95
Dialogue between religions, 206, 226
djinns, 197
Dodd, C. H., 132
Dubois, Abbé, 155
Dubs, Homer, 94
Duke of Lu, 125-26, 129
Dukkha, 118
Durga, 75

Eastern Christendom, 192
Edgerton, Franklin, 69n.
Eliade, Mircea, 61n.
Elizabeth II of England, 113
Emperor of Japan, 52n.
Epictetus, 16, 71
Eschaton, 150

E.S.P., 143
Evil, problem of, 84-85

Faith, 30
Fatima, 136
Fetish, 63
Filial piety, 110; see also Hsiao
Filson, F. V., 109
Four Noble Truths, 23, 45, 76-78, 101, 118, 120, 177, 180, 227
Frick, Heinrich, 226-28

Gandhi, Mohandas K., 102, 103, 107, 218
Garden of Eden, 80, 153
Gautama, see Buddha
Giles, Herbert, 49n., 81n.
God (defined), 19n.
Gödel, Dr. Kurt, 28-29
Goguel, Maurice, 131
Golden Rule
  biblical teaching, 92-93
  Confucian thought, in, 94-96
Gospel and other faiths, 223
Ground of Being, 34, 54, 55, 56
Guignebert, Charles, 131
Guillaume, Alfred, 140, 199
Gunas, 105

Hadith, 194, 198
Hall, Edward T., 207
Hara-kiri, 171
Hegirah (Hijrah), 137
Henley, William, 45
Hero, myth of the, 34
Hillel, Rabbi, 92, 228
Hilliard, F. H., 124n.
Hinduism
  basic world view, 21-22
  classes, 174, 217
  deity in, 41-43
  exclusiveness in, 217-18
  nonmissionary in nature, 173
  nonviolence in, 105-8
  salvation in, 69-76
  three margas, 70